AF412358

THE MISSION AND MESSAGE
OF
RAMALINGA SWAMY

The Mission and Message
of
Ramalinga Swamy

T. DAYANANDAN FRANCIS

MOTILAL BANARSIDASS PUBLISHERS
PRIVATE LIMITED
DELHI

First Edition: Delhi, 1990

© 1990 BY MOTILAL BANARSIDASS PUBLISHERS PVT. LTD.
ALL RIGHTS RESERVED.

ISBN: 81–208–0661–1 (Cloth)
ISBN: 81–208–0685–9 (Paper)

Also available at:

MOTILAL BANARSIDASS
Bungalow Road, Jawahar Nagar, Delhi 110 007
Chowk, Varanasi 221 001
Ashok Rajpath, Patna 800 004
24 Race Course Road, Bangalore 560 001
120 Royapettah High Road, Mylapore, Madras 600 004

DEDICATED

to the memory of

TAMIL PERIYĀR

TIRU. VI. KALAYANASUNDARANAR

(1883-1953)

an ardent follower and an able exponent of
the teachings of RAMALINGA SWAMY

ACKNOWLEDGEMENTS

The author acknowledges his thanks to the Christian Institute for the Study of Religion and Society, Bangalore, and the Christian Literature Society, Madras, for giving permission to bring out an enlarged version of the booklet published by them in 1972. He also wishes to thank Tanis, Monica, Joyce and Sweetlin for their help in typing the script for the press, and M/s. Motilal Banarsidass, Delhi for their willingness to publish this little book.

TDF

CONTENTS

I

THE MAN AND HIS WORK

A Revolutionary Thinker of the Nineteenth Century

Chidambaram Ramalinga Swamy who lived in the last century is acknowledged to be an outstanding saint and poet of Tamil Nadu. He has distinguished himself both as a revolutionary thinker and as a reformer. His main contribution to the religious life of the Tamils is his concept of *Śuddha Sanmārga* or *The True Path*. It points to a way of life which transcends the conventional patterns of religion. Ramalinga claims this path as being distinct from and higher than the Śaiva Siddhānta concept of *Sanmārga*,[1] as well as from the *Samarasa Sanmārga* or equality of all religions propagated in Tamil Nadu, chiefly by the Śaiva saint Tāyumānavar.

The Swamy made the ideals of *Jīvakāruṇyam* (charity towards all beings) and *Ānmaneya Orumaippāḍu* (oneness of the souls of all beings) the basis of his new path. Stressing the importance of these spiritual virtues he condemned the evils of casteism and religious bigotry. He considered them to be the main hindrances for Śuddha Sanmārga. No one has ever preached so vehemently against the evils of casteism and religious bigotry as Ramalinga, excepting perhaps Periyār E.V. Ramaswamy, the leader of the Dravida Kazhagam. Ramalinga's writings have been a source of inspiration to several of the reformers who came after him to fight against these evils in Tamil Nadu.

It is interesting to note that Ramalinga was a contemporary of Raja Ram Mohan Roy, Swami Dayananda Saraswati and Sri Ramakrishna Paramahamsa. Unlike those men, Ramalinga hailed

---

1 According to Śaiva Siddhānta, *Dāsamārga, Satputramārga* and *Sahamārga*, the three paths which represent *Caryā, Kriyā* and *Yoga*, are transcended by *Sanmārga* which represents the path of *jñāna*.

from the non-Brahmin circle. Like Dayananda and Paramahamsa, Ramalinga had no English education. He was well-versed in Tamil and the bulk of his writings is in verse form. The support and sympathy of the public in the case of Ramalinga were not so strong as in the case of the northern reformers. Further, Ramalinga's name has not received recognition outside Tamil Nadu. His writings, with the exception of a few poems, are yet to be rendered in English and other languages.

In the Line of the Śaiva Saints and Siddhas

It is important to view the life and work of the Swamy within the framework of Tamil Śaivism. The origin of Śaivism in Tamil Nadu is traced back to very early times. One of the terms used to denote god in *Tolgāppiam*,[1] the most ancient available grammar of Tamil, is *kandali*. It means 'One who is free from bonds'. Some scholars are of the opinion that the Tamils of that period were familiar with the Śaiva concept of human bondage. There are clear evidences in the *Sangam* literature (*circa* 100 B.C. to 200 A.D.) for the existence of the cult of Śiva. In *Śilappadigāram*, an epic poem written during this period, Lord Śiva is referred to as 'the great one who is free from birth'.[2]

It was in the sixth century that Śaivism gained momentum in Tamil Nadu. It became so powerful as to suppress the growth of Jainism and Buddhism. The most able exponents of Śaivism during this period were Saint Tirumūlar and Saint Tirunāvukkarasar. Tirumūlar's *Tirumandiram* is a great work of mystical wisdom. It consists of a little over three thousand stanzas. Tirumūlar, in this monumental work of his, deals with the fundamental doctrines of Siddhānta, together with their ethical implications. Tirunāvukkarasar also known as Appar has sung a number of lyrical poems in various metres. These are compiled together. The compilation is known as the *Tevāram* of Tirunāvukkarasar. Both the saints have expressed their mature thoughts about the oneness of the human race. They have condemned the evils of casteism and religious superstition. They have insisted

---

1 Scholars agree that the date of this book could not be later than second century B.C.

2 *piravā yākkaip periyōn*

on the worship of God in spirit and truth. The love of God and the love of fellowmen are emphasized in their writings to a great extent.

During the following three centuries saints like Sambandar, Sundarar and Māṇikkavāsagar made their valuable contributions to Śaivite devotional literature.

In the later part of the history of Śaivism in Tamil Nadu, the Siddhas had an important role to play. The Siddhas were people who were bestowed with *siddhis* or extraordinary powers. The Siddhas (Cittars) of Tamil Nadu were noted for their ability to perform miracles in the service of society. Their songs became popular among the masses. They have protested against the traditional mode of worship and religious observances. They were often mistaken for atheists and agnostics. But they have never deviated from the fundamental beliefs of Śaivism. Tirumular himself is said to have been a Siddha. Among the Siddhas, Paṭṭinattār, Badragiriyār, Pāmbāṭṭi Siddhar, Agappei Siddhar, Iḍaikkāṭṭu Siddhar and Sivavākkiyar are the more famous ones. The Siddhas are compared to the Sufis and the Gnostics.[1]

Saint Ramalinga was born and brought up in Śaivism. He was greatly influenced by the lives and writings of the Śaiva saints as well as the Siddhas. He acknowledges in his writings that he had accepted Sambandar as his guru. He has paid tributes to other saints as well. He has followed their line of thought in his compositions. He was immensely influenced by the *Tiruvāsagam* of Māṇikkavāsagar. He has written six cantos following the pattern of Māṇikkavāsagar and has given the same titles given in *Tiruvāsagam*.[2]

The influence of the Siddhas on the life of Ramalinga was also great. He is reported to have performed some miracles. Like several other Siddhas he was very much concerned about the glorious life without death. He was conscious of the fact that he was unmistakably in the line of the Śaiva saints and Siddhas. He sings: "My Lord, do I not belong to the illustrious line of

---

1 A.V. Subramania Iyer, *The Poetry and the Philosophy of the Tamil Siddhars*, p. 3.

2 An interesting study in comparison is made by A.S. Vazhittunairaman in his *Vaḷḷalārum Vāsagarum.*

your devotees who flourished in unintermittent succession like the plantains?"[1]

Ramalinga met with severe opposition from the orthodox Śaivites of his time. He was branded a heretic and was called a pseudo-teacher of Śaivism for his radical thinking and new teaching. He built a place of worship entirely different in structure from that of the Śaiva temple and placed a light in the place of the idol. Some of his modern disciples contend that he broke away completely with Śaivism. But this is not quite true. A careful examination of his teachings would reveal his faithfulness to the fundamental doctrine of Śaivism. The bulk of his poems and lyrics is in praise of Lord Śiva. While accepting the lofty ideals of Śaivism, he ventured to show the 'more excellent way' along the lines of love and compassion. Thus he made the path of salvation accessible to the masses.

---

1 Translation by P. Mutharasu in *Hymns of Tiruvaruṭpā*, p.73.

II

THE LIFE OF RAMALINGA

The Announcement of His Birth

Ramalinga was born on the fifth of October 1823 at Marudhur, a place near Chidambaram. A Śiva yogi is said to have predicted his birth to his mother saying, "You shall give birth to a son who will become great. He will do good to humanity by establishing *Sanmārga*." His *jātaka* (horoscope) describes him as *Cirañjīvī*—one who will never die and will be hailed by the people of the world as *Vaḷḷal* or 'all-giver'. It is further stated in his *jātaka* that at the age of ten he would realize in himself the traits of a reformer through *śakti*, while at thirty he would attain freedom from the chain of birth, and become a *Kaivalya* at forty. At fifty he would obtain *Prāṇadēha* (imperishable body) of a Siddha.

Ramalinga states the purpose of his birth in one of his later verses: "It is to correct the people of the world whose heart is full of darkness and to gain for them admission into the Sanmārga Sangam and thus make it possible for them the experience of heaven here and now that God has sent me in this *yuga*, charged with his divine grace". (5485)[1]

At the Temple

When Ramalinga was a baby he was taken by his parents to the temple at Chidambaram. It is said that the baby was fascinated by the vision of Naṭarāja and it burst into laughter. The priest at once remarked to Ramalinga's father, "Your son has received the divine vision and grace; he is born for something great with the grace of God inherent in him".

---

1 The numbers refer to the order followed in *Tiruvaruṭpā*, (ed.) Ooran Adigal, Vadalur: Samarasa Sanmarga Aaraicci Nilayam, 1972.

Unless otherwise stated the translations are by the author.

A month after this incident Ramalinga's father died. The family moved to Ponneri, a place near Madras. Sabapathy Pillai, the elder brother of Ramalinga, assumed the responsibilities for the family. He was a Tamil scholar and earned his livelihood by delivering lectures and discourses on the *Purāṇas*.

Too Great to be Taught.......

Ramalinga received his primary education from his brother. But he did not give proper attention to his studies. So Sabapathy sent him to his own teacher Kanchi Sabapathy Mudaliar. Ramalinga did not make any progress and neglected his studies. He spent much of his time at Kandakrōṭṭam, a temple of Muruga.[1] Ramalinga's teacher overheard his songs and was struck with reverence and wonder at the profound knowledge and devotion of his student. He thought that he was too small to be his teacher and informed his brother that Ramalinga needed no longer to be his pupil.

Sabapathy, however, was annoyed at his brother's indifference to studies. He ordered his wife not to give Ramalinga food and clothing. Ramalinga's sister-in-law had motherly affection for him and so it was difficult for her to carry out the orders of her husband. She advised Ramalinga to enter the house by the back door and have his food when his brother was away. She also entreated Ramalinga with tears and kind words to take his studies seriously. Ramalinga was moved by her words and promised her that he would remain in the house and study the lessons. He requested that a separate room be given to him where he could have his private prayers. His brother gave him a room upstairs.

Vision of Muruga in the Upper Room

Ramalinga hung up a mirror on one of the walls of the room and decorated it with flowers. He lit an oil lamp before it. He also burnt incense and camphor in front of it. The spear-like image of the flame in the mirror enabled him to contemplate deeply on Muruga.[2] This kind of worship and meditation went on for several

---

1   Although Muruga is depicted as the younger son of Śiva in the *Purāṇas*, he represents a divine form of Śiva.

2 Muruga holds a spear (*vēel*) in his hand. It is interpreted as *śakti* and *jñāna*.

days. One day the divine form of Muruga was visible to his eyes in the mirror. Ramalinga was only nine years old then. The incident had an abiding influence on Ramalinga. It led him to think of God as light and to introduce the mirror and lamp in the place of idols in the sanctuary he built later at Vadalur.

Ramalinga tells in his writings that at this early age he was initiated into the learning of scriptures, literature and grammar without the intermediary of a human teacher. He sings to his Lord: "Thou hast given me understanding of Truth without the intermediary of a teacher in such measure that the learned ones come to me to learn of Thee." He also tells of an experience in which he was specially blessed by Muruga who said in his ears a divine message and entered into him. This is said to have happened at the temple at Tiruvotriyur, a place near Madras. He often tells in his verses that Jñānasambandar, one among the Samaya Ācāryas of Śaivism, who lived twelve centuries before him, was in fact his guru. Ramalinga further believed that Jñānasambandar was the incarnation of Muruga himself.

Young Ramalinga Delivers a Discourse

Ramalinga at this early stage is said to have delivered an excellent discourse on a passage in *Periapurāṇam*.[1] He was sent in the place of his brother who had fallen ill. The passage that was to be expounded was the life history of Jñānasambandar, the spiritual guru of Ramalinga. Ramalinga started the discourse and continued until midnight, explaining only two lines in the first stanza. There was great astonishment on the part of the audience and Ramalinga was requested to continue the discourse on Jñānasambandar in the following weeks. This event stands as an important one in the life of Ramalinga as it brought him out of the seclusion of his room into the wider world.

Sabapathy gradually understood that his brother was indeed a seer. His attitude to him changed to one of adoration.

---

1 The twelfth book of *Śaiva Tirumurai* or Devotional Poetry. In it is recorded the biography of sixty-three Nāyanmārs. The work belongs to the twelfth century A.D. Its author is Sēkiḷār. The entire book is in verse form.

"Here Goes the Man!"

During this time Ramalinga used to make his daily visits to the temple at Tiruvotriyūr. His biographers have recorded several mystical incidents connected with his visits to the temple. One incident is to this effect: There was a saṃnyāsī lying on the verandah of a house in the Main Car Street leading to the temple. He would abuse all those who passed by, using words like donkey, bull etc. No one dared to go near him and stop him from this. When he saw Ramalinga passing, he exclaimed, "Here goes the man'" Ramalinga went near him and whispered something in his ears. The saṃnyāsī left the place for good.

Early Writings

Ramalinga wrote a number of lyrics and poems during this period. One of his best compositions, *Ingittamālai* was written at this time. It was written in the form of a dialogue between a husband and his wife, who are none other than God and the individual soul. Ramalinga attempted prose writing also during this early period of his life. He produced a book on justice. It was based on the story of the ancient Tamil king Manu Nīdi Colan. The book was commended by several Tamil scholars of the day. By this time Ramalinga had gathered round him a small circle of friends and disciples—which included his former teacher Kanchi Sabapathy Mudaliar.

Desire for Ascetic Life

Ramalinga's brother wanted him to get married. He was persuaded to accept the proposal. It is recorded that he spent the first night of his wedded life in reading *Tiruvāsagam* with his wife. He never tried the life of a married man. He desired the life of an ascetic from his young age and led a life of simplicity and humility. In one of his poems he says that he would hold his hands folded while walking and cover his body with two pieces of white cloth. He feared to sit on a high pedestal and cross his legs in a majestic manner. He was afraid to sing aloud and would not sleep on a soft bed. He had no desire for money and as a sign of his disdain for wealth would often throw coins in ponds and tanks. (3454; 3461) In this he resembled Ramakrishna Paramahamsa. Ramalinga did not like living in Madras. He hated city life. He liked spending his time in meditation in rural and forest areas.

Finally he decided to leave Madras and make a pilgrimage to some of the sacred places in Tamil Nadu. Some friends of his accompanied him. The pilgrimage was undertaken by foot. He visited Kanjipuram, Chidambaram, Sirkali and several other places. Accepting the invitation of a friend he came to Karunguli, a village near Chidambaram.

Nine Years at Karunguli

Ramalinga came to Karunguli in 1858. He was thirty-five then. He stayed there for nine years. During this period he wrote a number of lyrics and poems. He preached to his disciples and to people who lived in Karunguli and the nearby villages. The theme of his preaching was love and compassion towards all beings. He made his message simple so that the illiterate people could follow it without any difficulty. He appealed to the people who came to him to give up meat-eating. He also pointed out the importance of devotion to God for attaining grace. Learned men and orthodox Śaivites would often come to him to hold debates and ask questions, some to learn and others to criticise. Ramalinga used to answer their questions patiently and argue with them in such a manner as to give a clear exposition of his teachings. He is said to have performed several miracles during the years he spent at Karunguli. Once he cured a man who was suffering from leprosy by giving him a pinch of sacred ashes. He also cured a man afflicted with a chronic eye disease, and the man recovered his lost eyesight.

By this time many became the disciples of Ramalinga. Ramalinga looked different from the traditional Śaivite ascetics. He did not wear saffron coloured clothes. He wore a white robe. He was short and thin and had a sorrowful look in his eyes. His biographers say that he had attained the imperishable *svarṇa deha* or golden body of a Siddha by then. Photographers could not take his picture although they attempted to do so on eight occasions.

Founding of the Sangam

Convinced that a society should be set up for spreading his message of compassion to all living beings (*Jīvakāruṇyam*) and the principles of his True Path (*Sanmārga*), he established in 1865 the *Samarasa Śuddha Sanmārga Sangam*. Membership was open to all who had compassion towards living beings and who vowed to abstain from killing and flesh-eating. No restrictions were imposed on the basis of caste, creed, religion or nationality. Provision was made for flesh-eaters to be 'outer members' till they gave it up. Ramalinga wrote in a pamphlet that the president of the *Sangam* was the Lord himself and all those who have *aruḷ* or compassion were its members.

The main objectives of the *Sangam* as pointed out in the writings of Ramalinga are as follows:

1. Teaching and practice of *Jīvakāruṇyam*.
2. Abolishing meat-eating, temple sacrifices and superstitious beliefs.
3. Casting away *jāti* and *varṇa* (caste) differences and bringing about unity among people of all creeds by making them realize the oneness of all souls in love. (*Ānmanēya orumaippāḍu*).
4. Inculcation of the glorious life without death.

Ministry at Vadalur

In 1866 Ramalinga made Parvathipuram, a nearby village, his centre of activities. It came to be known as Vadalur. The first thing that Ramalinga did when he moved to this place was the building of a charity home. He built it up with the help of his wealthy friends and named it *Sattiya Dharmasālai*. It was his strong conviction that physical poverty should be removed before making any attempt to feed people with spiritual food.

On inaugurating the Dharmasālai, Ramalinga read out to the people his treatise on *Jīvakāruṇyam*.[1] It explains the main features of the concept in logical sequence. The Dharmasālai is still functioning at Vadalur.

Ramalinga started a training centre for the *Sanmārga sevaks*. It was named *Samarasa Vēda Pāḍasālai*. Similarly, a school for children was run on the campus of the Dharmasālai. It is interesting to note that Ramalinga made arrangements for instruction to be given to children in Tamil, Sanskrit and English.

1　It was later included in his *Tiruvaruṭpā*.

Songs of Divine Grace

In the following year a collection of his poems which forms the first four parts of his *Tiruvaruṭpā* (Songs of Divine Grace) was published by some of his disciples on behalf of the *Sangam*. Ramalinga never wanted the concluding part of his work to be published. He believed that the truths mentioned in it were specially meant for the inner circle of his disciples.

Ramalinga's poems and lyrics are written in chaste Tamil and they reveal his mystical as well as his revolutionary thinking. *Tiruvaruṭpā* contains about 7,000 poems. The book is divided into six parts. It includes the poems he wrote for the inner circle. A few selected poems are given below in English translation.[1]

GOD CAUGHT IN LOVE

My Lord! you are very great like a mountain, but you come within the handgrip called Love. You are a great king who enters into the small hut called devotion. You are the (priceless) treasure that is caught in the net called Love... You are very great and unfathomable like an ocean, but you abide in the small pot called Love...You are the effulgent lustre that abides even in a small atom. You are the almighty Śiva who is the very incarnation of Love.[2]   (3269)

A MISERABLE OFFENDER I AM

All your devotees sing your praise in sweet music; they worship at your feet; they look continuously at the indescribable beauty of your form, feast their eyes, exult in the immeasurable joy at heart, pour forth torrents of tears from their eyes and dance in that ecstasy. They reflect incessantly on your grace and cry, 'My father', but I, a sinner, am much vexed by my fraudulent mind; alas! What am I to do with it?[3]   (601)

TAKE ME TO YOUR BOSOM

If a father takes to task his mischievous son, the boy's mother

---

1 An elaborate presentation is made in chapter three.
2 Translation by Mutharasu.
3 Translation by Mutharasu.

will come to his rescue; if on the other hand, the mother punishes him for his faults, the father will console the boy. But I have, for my father and mother, none but you, my Lord! ... I am completely exhausted; it is enough, please stop punishing me any further; but embrace me with all your grace.[1]   (3386)

A Petition to the Lord

...Please grant me the acquaintance of the good that concentrate all their thoughts on your lotus-like feet with unparalleled devotion; give me the power to shun the association of those whose thoughts and words differ; make me extol your glory and refrain from saying falsehood; direct me to tread the righteous path; save me from being grappled by the devil of religious fanaticism; help me to forget completely the desire for women; and never to forget thee; shower on me the pure knowledge and the wealth of your grace so as to enable me to live a full and eternal life free from disease.[2]   (8)

Life and Service for Your Glory

O, my father, this is my appeal. Please hear and grant it to me. I must love all living beings and serve them. I must traverse the length and breadth of the entire world and proclaim your glory and grace. I must wield the sceptre of your gracious light so that the true path of *Sanmārgam* which occupies an ineffably supreme position, may flourish everywhere. You must also forgive me, if I commit any mistake, unaware, in my enthusiasm; and grant me that state of inseparable union with you, my Lord.[3]   (4079)

Reverence for Life

...Whenever I saw crops withering for want of rain, my heart did wither too. When I happened to see poor people exhausted and worn out due to starvation for days together, even after begging at every door with their hunger never satisfied, my

---

1, 2, 3 Translation by Mutharasu.

heart throbbed fearfully obsessed by grief. When I came across
people suffering for a long time from incurable and chronic
diseases, I was agonised. When I met people spotlessly honour-
able but totally depressed on account of poverty, I also got
depressed.[1] (3471)

THE WISDOM OF DEATHLESSNESS

The four *Vedas*, the *Āgamas* and all the *Śāstras* do not become
our own wisdom, but remain only outside ourselves as our
wisdom for the market. By experiencing the Absolute, the
Lord Beyond, I have come to learn the wisdom of deathlessness.[2] (5295)

RETURN TO THE LORD

In castes, in philosophical dogmas, in the ceremonials of
sectarian practices, in the noisy debates on *Śāstras*, in the wars
of *Gotras*—
Pinning your faith in these differences, distinctions and quarrels
from times immemorial, you men and women of the world are
restless and tossed about hither and thither...
The Lord... is now coming to open and in the broad daylight
of our experience will play his unique game of glory and
grace.
It is therefore time for you to turn this way. And I do call you
all, men and women of the world, in the name of our Lord and
Master, to your ineffable destiny of perfection.[3] (5566)

Satya Jñāna Sabai

Ramalinga had been making plans for the building of a place of
worship. He drew up the plan for its construction with his own
hand and gave it to his disciples and asked them to erect the
structure. The building was completed in 1871 and was opened
for worship. Ramalinga named it Satya Jñāna Sabai (Hall of True
Wisdom). It was designed in the shape of a full-blown lotus
flower representing the human body, the temple of God. A mirror

---

1 Translation by Mutharasu.
2, 3 Translation by Balakrishnan.

and an oil lamp were installed in the sanctuary. Seven curtains were put in front of the glass. They represented the seven *śaktis*, the veils of illusion. Every year on Taipūsam[1] the curtains were to be removed one by one so as to have a clear vision of the lamp in the glass, shining in splendour. The implication is that *Śuddha Śivam* or *Para Śivam* could be seen only after passing beyond these *śaktis* of illusion. The *Jyəti Darśan* continues till today. On Taipūsam day thousands of people crowd at Vadalur.

Opposition from the Orthodox Śaivites

Ramalinga's fame spread all over Tamil Nadu and people flocked to Vadalur from far and near. Orthodox Śaivites were watching the activities of Ramalinga and the *Sangam* with suspicion and hatred. The publication of Ramalinga's work under the title *Tiruvaruṭpā* aroused their fury. The title, they contended, was applicable only to their twelve canonical devotional books (*Tirumurais*). They branded Ramalinga a heretic and blasphemer. Their hatred grew all the more when they found the lyrics and poems of Ramalinga being sung in homes, schools and temples, sometimes replacing the singing of *Tēvaram* and *Tiruvāsagam*. They began to abuse Ramalinga openly and told the people that he can by no means be regarded as a Samaya Ācārya and given equal status with the authors of the canonical books. Further, they found fault with Ramalinga's title *Vaḷḷalār*. Although Ramalinga did not apply the title to himself, he was criticised as one who considered himself equal to God by allowing such a title to be applied to himself. Another serious charge brought against Ramalinga was that he built the Satya Jñāna Sabai as a rival to the Sabai at Chidambaram.

The opposition came chiefly from the great maḍādipatis (Heads of maḍams or monasteries) of Tiruvannamalai, Tiruvaduthurai and Dharmapuram.

Armuga Nāvalar, a great Tamil scholar and staunch Śaivite of Jaffna, was in Tamil Nadu at that time and he was instigated by the heads of the maḍams to fight against Ramalinga. He started abusing Ramlinga in public meetings, and he wrote booklets criti-

---

1   Special pūjā offered in the month of Tai. It takes place in January.

cising him. He ridiculed Ramalinga's work *Aruṭpā* (verses of grace) as *Maruṭpā* (verses of fear). He also filed a suit against Ramalinga and dragged him to the court. Ramalinga defended himself and won the case.

However, the debate over his person and work continued for over two years. During this period a number of pamphlets were written and published by his enemies condemning Ramalinga and his writings. Some of them were answered by his disciples.

Ramalinga was deeply wounded in heart. He felt sorry for having engaged himself in this controversy. In a verse written at that time, he invites his adversaries in touching words to forget all hatred and join him:

> O ye men of controversy, please listen to me. Do not waste your time. Learn to admire and praise the dance of the Lord in the sabai of grace. He will not reject you for your evil words. Instead, he will receive you. These are not words of deception. I tell these for your own good since I consider you as my kith and kin.[1] (5454)

Mistaken for a Miracle-maker

Ramalinga was disappointed when people misunderstood and misinterpreted his abilities in performing miracles as a Siddha. People began to crowd around him in large numbers with the only intention of witnessing the miracles. Many wanted to get benefited by those miracles. They began even to bring the dead to Vadalur. Some of the evil disciples of Ramalinga started collecting money from the people promising cures and blessings without the knowledge of their master.

A Danish missionary, C. Ochs, who visited the area in 1871 writes in a letter published in the 'Danish Missions Blad' (*Danish Missionary Journal*, 1872, p. 52) as follows:

> At Vadalur a swindler is going around these days. He pretends to be able to raise the dead. The missionary at Pannurutti told me that in these days this man shall perform the trick which he has promised for a long time. People are coming from far-

---

1 Translation by Mutharasu.

off places to see him. He is in a hurry to perform this miracle. Recently his booty was stolen by thieves. Now he wants to make the lost money by deceiving people ... In Pannurutti, a man who was dying is reported to have ordered his wife not to cremate his body but instead to send a sum of money to the miracle-maker so that he would raise him to life when he had died.[1]

Ramalinga does speak in his poems about the dead being raised and prays God to grant him the gift of restoring life to the dead. One verse runs like this:

O gracious light that showed the ability to make all the dead rise with joy, grant me, I pray, that virtue which would empower me to raise the dead at my wish and bidding.   (4082)

Elsewhere he says that he prayed for a never-decaying body, destructible neither by the five elements nor by the Lord of Death, and says that he was granted the boon. (5460) But he never attempted to raise the dead. He only preached that by following *Śuddha Sanmārga* and *Jīvakāruṇyam* the imperishable body of a Siddha could be obtained.

The gross misunderstanding on the part of the people made him write a public appeal in 1873, requesting them not to be deceived by the rumour that a miracle was to take place at Vadalur on 20-9-1873. In the concluding lines of the appeal we have these words:

We are not sure whether a miracle is going to take place or not; nor can we be sure of its happening now or at some other time in the future. So be on your guard and do not be deceived.

The Closing of the Sabai

Ramalinga was further disappointed when he found his followers slipping away from the ideals of *Śuddha Sanmārga*. He noticed a growing tendency among them to regard him as a demigod. Ramalinga strongly rebuked them for this. In a verse addressed to the members of the *Sangam* he says:

---

1 Translation from Danish by Dr. Kaj Baago, formerly of the United Theological College, Bangalore.

Please listen to me, ye men of *Sanmārga Sangam*. I speak, prostrating myself at your feet. *Only consider me as one among you. Worship only the God Almighty.* Do not speak in the fashion of people who profess false religions and spoil your wisdom.
(5452)

The indisciplined life of his followers and the disappointing behaviour of people in general to his teachings were most painful to him. In 1873 he ordered the Jñāna Sabai building to be locked up and he kept the keys with himself. He is reported to have said the following words to those who were around him at that time:

You are not worthy to be members of the *Sangam*. The real members of the *Sangam* are living far away in the north. You do not follow the principles of my teachings. It appears that you are determined not to be convinced by me. Before long some people from Russia and America and other foreign countries will come to this land and preach to you the same doctrine of universal love and brotherhood that I have all along preached to you. Then you will know and appreciate the great truths which I have been vainly trying to put before you. You will also find the brothers from the north doing many wonders in India.

Final Discourse and Samādhi

After closing the Sabai, Ramalinga made his abode in a nearby village called Mettukkuppam. He stayed there in a small hut which he named *Siddhi Viḷāgam* (Abode of Siddhi). Soon he decided to get absorbed in *yoga nittirai* or *samādhi*. On 30th January 1874 Ramalinga delivered his final discourse to his disciples. He said:

Friends, I opened a shop but there was none to purchase; so I have closed it. I will not be visible to your eyes for a certain period, although I will be universally present in the world. My imperishable body will enter into the bodies of all living beings. I will reappear again at the proper time after having preached my message in other countries. Till then take to the path of *Jīvakāruṇyam*. Worship God in the form of light and attain salvation.

Ramalinga went into his room and stretched himself on a carpet. He gave orders that the room be locked from outside. He had already told his disciples not to open the room and not to be disappointed as he would not be visible to their eyes. He also told them that if the government officers ordered the door to be opened, there was no need to fear, for by the grace of God nothing would be found in the room.

The news of the miraculous disappearance of Ramalinga spread everywhere. The local police reported the matter to higher authorities suspecting foul play. J.H. Garstin, I.C.S., the then Collector of South Arcot District came to the spot and made an enquiry. He did not order the room to be opened. Instead he contributed twenty rupees for a feast to the poor arranged in memory of Ramalinga. He also wrote a few lines about Ramalinga in the *South Arcot District Manual* published in 1878 and it was later reprinted in the *South Arcot District Gazetteer* in 1906. The following is an extract from the collector's report:

> ... In 1874, he locked himself in a room (still in existence in Mettukuppam, hamlet of Karunguli) which he used for samadhi or mystic meditation, and instructed his disciples not to open it for some time. He has never been seen since and the room is still locked. It is held by those who still believe in him that he was miraculously made one with his God and that in the fullness of time he will reappear to the faithful.

The report concludes with these words:

> Whatever may be thought of his claims to be a religious leader, it is generally admitted, by those who are judges of such matters, that his poems, many of which have been published, stand on a high plane, and his story is worth noting as an indication of the directions which religious fervour may still take.

Ramalinga is said to have granted visions to several of his disciples during the period that immediately followed his miraculous disappearance.

Forerunner of the Theosophical Society

Tholuvūr Velayutham Mudaliar was one among the leading

disciples of Ramalinga. He was serving in the Tamil department of the Presidency College, Madras. He gave a statement to the Theosophical Society regarding the life and work of Ramalinga. He quoted Ramalinga's prophecy concerning the coming of persons from Russia and America after him to preach the same gospel he preached. He concludes his statement in the following words:

> This prophecy has, in my opinion, just been literally fulfilled. The fact that the Mahatmas in the North exist, is no new idea to us as Hindus; and the strange fact that the advent of Madame Blavatsky and Colonel Olcott from Russia and America was foretold several years before they came to India, is an incontrovertible proof that my Guru was in communication with those Mahatmas under whose direction the Theosophical Society was subsequently founded.[1]

This statement was published in the journal *The Theosophist* (July, 1882) with an editorial comment by H.P. Blavatsky:

> This is one of those cases of previous foretelling of a coming event which is least of all open to suspicion of bad faith. The honourable character of the witness, the wide publicity of his Guru's monuments, and the impossibility that he could have got from public rumour, or the journals of the day, any intimation that the Theosophical Society would be formed and would operate in India—all these conspire to support the inference that Ramalingam Yogi was verily in the counsels of those who ordered us to found the society. In March 1873, we were directed to proceed from Russia to Paris. In June we were told to proceed to the United States where we arrived on July 6th ... This was the very time when Ramalingam was most forcibly prefiguring the events which should happen...

The Second Coming of Ramalinga

Since Ramalinga had stated in his final discourse that he would reappear again at the proper time, after having preached his message in other countries, several of his followers sincerely believe that his second coming will take place in history. M.P. Sivagnanam,

---

1 This statement is found in *Hints on Esoteric Theosophy*.

in his biography of Ramalinga, sees this second coming in the advent of Mahatma Gandhi who also came from the North and who was born in the month of October as was Ramalinga. Further, Gandhi died on January 30, 1948 the same date on which Swamy Ramalinga attained Samādhi seventy-four years ago.[1]

However, most of the modern disciples and biographers of Ramalinga do not give any importance to his second coming. Ooran Aḍigaḷ who has written the most recent biography of Ramalinga, in his monumental work says the following words regarding his second coming: "My answer to the question Will Vaḷḷalār (Ramalinga) come again? is this. No one talks about saints like Jñānasambandar coming again. So also there is no need for talk about the Swamy's second coming".[2]

But Ooran Aḍigaḷ firmly believes that Ramalinga was born in previous birth as Tāyumānavar, who was a great Śaiva saint of Tamil Nadu.[3] He was a philosophical poet and he had discoursed at length on the equality of all religions. He lived about two hundred and fifty years before Ramalinga.

---

1 M.P. Sivagnanam, *Vaḷḷalār Kaṇḍa Orumaippāḍu.*
2 Ooran Aḍigaḷ, *Ramalinga Aḍigaḷ Varalāṟu,* Vadalur: Samarasa Sanmarga Aaraicci Nilayam, Appendix 8, p. 39.
3 *Ibid.,* Appendix 7, pp. 31-33.

III

THE MISSION AND MESSAGE OF RAMALINGA SWAMY

The Teachings of the Tamil Siddhas

As observed earlier, Ramalinga Swamy has acknowledged his indebtedness to the Tamil Siddhas by identifying himself as one coming in the unintermittent succession of the Siddhas. The teachings of the Siddhas provide proper perspective for understanding the inner experience as well as the socio-religious spirituality commended by Ramalinga Swamy in his writings. The message of the Tamil Siddhas is based on the direct experience of God over against the cultic beliefs and practices of their times. Most of them lived during the 10th and 15th century A.D. Tirumūlar, the author of *Tirumandiram,* probably lived during the 6th and 7th century A.D. He is supposed to be the oldest of all the Siddhas and his poems surpass the writings of other siddhas both in number and quality.

The Tamil Siddhas are said to be 18 in number, but many others are also considered to be Siddhas. Several of them belong to a later age. Their poetical works, in most cases, belong to medicine, alchemy, astrology and yoga. Kailasapathy thinks that the number 18 itself had some mystical significance. *Gorakhanāth,* one of the chief Nāth Yogis, appears in the list. The 18 Siddhas are: Śiva Vākkiar, Paṭṭinattār, Pattiragiriyār, Pāmbāṭṭi Cittar, Iḍaikāttu Cittar, Agappēyar, Kudumbaiār, Kaḍuveḷiār, Aḷugaṇiār, Konganār, Cattai Muni, Tiruvaḷḷuvar, Agattiar, Tirumūlar, Subramaṇiar, Vālmīgar, Rāmadēvar, and Karuvūrar. Among these, the first 8 are the popular ones while Tirumūlar is held in high esteem as literary and religious genius. The name Karuvūrar is very similar to Karuvūrtēvar, author of one of the 12 Śaivite *Tirumurais*.[1]

The Tamil Siddhas have their counterparts in the Vacanakāras of Viraśaivism. The poems of the Bauls of Bengal, Kabīr and his followers are very similar to the message of the Tamil Siddhas. The Siddhas were revolutionaries in that they challenged the authority of the scriptures and condemned ritualistic ceremonies and the caste system in particular. Several of them hailed from low castes and they were well accepted by the people. Although the origin and substance of their teachings are often considered to be Tantric, many of them have deviated from the basic tantric principles of sexuality and have adopted the language of the *bhakti* cult to a considerable extent. Several of them preferred to use simple language and so invented and introduced popular literary style. Kailasapathy observes: "In terms of literary crafts and conventions, the Siddhas revolutionised Tamil poetry especially religio-philosophic poetry by bringing into the world the language of folklore. This bold device became irrevocable."[2] Kamil Zvelebil rightly points out that their language "is more often than not almost vulgar; at any rate it is a simple, colloquial idiom, close to the speech of the masses."[3]

The Cittars and Religious Awareness

The *Cittars* speak of their religious experience chiefly from the yogic point of view. Excepting *Agappēyar* and *Kaḍuveḷiyār* all others speak of yoga or Śiva-yoga. They are never tired of repeating the methods prescribed for raising the *kuṇḍalinī* from *mūlā-dhāram* through the six circles. But their writings are not completely free from presenting the inner experience with *bhakti* overtones. Some of the prominent *cittars* like *Tirumūlar, Tāyumānavar* and *Paṭṭinattār* were well versed in *bhakti* terminology. Their poems abound in *bhakti* ideas. Some of their verses stand on equal par

---

1   An account of the Tamil Cittars is found in *The Poets of Power*, London: Rider & Company, 1973. A similar presentation is found in A.V. Subramania Aiyer's *The Poetry and Philosophy of the Tamil Siddhas*, Chidambaram: Manivasagar Noolagam, 1969, pp. 47, 48.

2   Tamil Siddhas in *The Sants*, Schomer & Mcleod, (eds.), New Delhi: Motilal Banarsidass, 1987, p. 399.

3   *Op. cit.*, p. 21.

with those of the great Śaivite poets of Tamil Nadu. While speaking about their religious awareness the *cittars* chiefly emphasize the immanence of God in man, the mystical union with God and the charismatic gifts obtained by them by following the mystical yogic path.[1]

(a) *The Indwelling of God:* Primary importance is given to the knowledge of the indwelling God. The divine indwelling is often stated by them as the 'inner light'. In a sense the *cittars* are the Quakers of Tamil Nadu. The chief exponent of the 'inner light' in simple verse form is Śivavākkiyar. His verses are powerful and persuasive. While speaking about the vain search made by people for attaining the divine light he sings:

> Millions and millions of people
> have run all along
> seeking, searching and looking for
> the light that is within!
> Getting completely exhausted
> they die at last. (3)

> The light is not in heaven;
> it is in our own selves. (497)

He describes the inner light as 'the light that raises from the basic vein' (18). In another verse he refers to it as 'the light of knowledge'. "This light", he says, "if meditated upon for four *nāligai* (four minutes) by a yogi will enable him to renew his youth and supreme Brahmanhood" (68). According to him a true yogi is 'one who blows fire' in the yogic fashion (175, 185). He proclaims that once the compartment of fire in man (*nerup-parai*) is opened, he attains divinity. (122)

> I was in such a state
> that I did not know
> the One in me!
> Now that I have known
> the same, the indwelling One,

---

1 The numbers refer to *Cittar Pāḍalgaḷ*, Aru. Ramanathan (ed) Madras: Prema Prasuram, 1970.

who can see the One in me?
I have known him
deep, deep in my heart.   (6)

I do not have anybody in my heart
excepting God and myself.   (90)

He is hiding himself in me   (293)

See, he is in you as your watchman.   (126)

Iḍaikkāḍar speaks of this light as 'the true lamp within' when
he sings:

Why do you stumble
You fool,
When you have the true lamp
Within your own self?
Your state is akin
to those who would get drowned
in the sea
despite their holding
a lamp in hand   (74)

Similarly, some other *cittars* qualify the light within variously in
their poems. Tirumūlar calls it 'the light as the base' (*mūlatāra
jōti*). Tāyumāṇavar speaks of the yogic fire as 'the flame at the
base' (*mūlakkanal*).

The inner light is also referred to in terms which have no particular association with the symbol of light. Paṭṭinattār calls it 'the
basic seed (*mūlavittu*) while Pāmbāṭṭiyār uses the expression 'basic
root' (*mūlavēr*).

Tirumūlar views the divine light both in its transcendental and
immanent aspects. He calls the former 'the natural divine light'
(*āṇavilakkoḷi*). The latter is said to be seen in three stages while
practising yoga. The first stage represents the light seen as the
basic light in the base of the body (*mūlātāram*) when the yogi sits
in the yogic posture. It is called *mūlaviḷakkoḷi*. It should be noted
that the yogic processes Tirumūlar speaks of are related to Śiva-
yoga. He equates the inner light in all the three stages with Śivam.

The Śiva-yogis reach the splendid inner light and thus obtain
mukti. Tirumūlar says:

> They (Śiva-yogis) use the thrity-six *tattvas* as
> ladder steps for *mukti* state and do reach the
> splendid inner light. They see for themselves
> the indescribable Śivam and with clear
> knowledge they meditate being seated firmly as
> Śivam itself.   (170)

Sivavākkiyar in his exposition of Śiva-yoga equates the inner
yogic light with the five letters of *Śivāyanama*. The five letters rise
from the base circle (*mūlavaṭṭam*).

> The fire comes out
> rising from the five letters
> that have emerged from
> the basic circle.   (469)

Similarly the sacred dance of Śiva is related to the inner light
that is raised up within the body through the middle nerve (*naḍunāḍi*) or *suṣupti*. Tirumūlar states this experience as follows:

> Going through the middle nerve
> to the top of the head
> from where
> the ambrosia of moon
> flows unceasingly,
> I saw him who is
> the blissful light eternal.
> He performs his sacred dance
> in the blissful hall divine.   (569)

Pāmbāṭṭiyār declares that he has reached the highest stage of
obtaining the feet of Śiva through the knowing and raising of the
inner light:

> Raise slowly the heat and
> direct it in the stream
> that runs through the street.
> Then,

dance my dear snake!
Since we have reached his feet
having sought the divine light
between the eyebrows
above the nose.   (115)

(a) *naḍunāḍi* or *suṣupti*

Experiencing the inner light to the full includes drinking of
ambrosia which is called the nectar of moon. The *cittars* refer to
it as *madiyamudam* and *Semmadippāl*. It is said to be oozing between the Śiva-yogi's eyebrows.

(b) *Mystical Union*

The *cittars* speak of the mystical union with God in Advaitic
as well as Śaivite terminology. Paṭṭiṇattār describes his mystical
union with God thus:

I am you and
you are me indeed
when we two become one!
O Lord of perfection
You are ever sweet
like the taste of honey.   (*Pūraṇamālai* 100)

Addressing his own heart he sings:

My heart, you are merged now
with that which has
no name and address
light and space
and qualities of any kind.

                                        (*Nenjoḍu Magiḻdal,* 9)

You are merged with that, my heart,
which fills every place by its very self
as feeling and intellect.   (2)

You have reached the place
that cannot be described.   (26)

The *vāsana, yoga* and
the sphere of utter speechlessness
have gone.
Now my heart,
You have reached that state
which has no differentiation
whatsoever.   (30)

Pattiragiriyār longs for this state in his long poem of lamentation:

When shall I know
the truth of *mukti* state
from within my soul
that is said to be *advaita* like?   (202)

When shall I know in my heart
that you are yourself
and I am myself and thus
we are two while you are
the One as well?   (192)

When shall I be One with you
and remain in the same state
having you abide in me?   (160)

When shall I surrender myself to him
knowing through the eye of knowledge
that the present differentiation of 'I' and 'He'
and realize myself becoming one with himself.   (720)

The verses quoted above from Paṭṭinattār and Pattiragiriyār lend themselves for both non-dualistic and theistic interpretations. Several verses like the one given below bring out the theistic nature of the union typically expounded in Śaiva Siddhānta:

When shall I stand absorbed
under your gracious feet
leaving and forgetting the body
the store house of filth and worms?   (40)

The mystical union is said to be the state that transcends the knowledge gained by *Vedas* and *Śāstras*:

Pattiragiriyār puts it thus:

> When shall I see for myself
> the great mystery
> which is not found by the four Vedas
> although they searched for the same.   (48)

Kudambaiyār puts the same idea in a verse when he sings:

> Will any written bond
> be of any use
> to those who rely on
> the open space for truth?   (8)

Kudambaiyār subordinates everything else to the highest of union with God. In the following verses, however, some *cittars* like Iḍaikkāḍar and Agappēyar make clear reference to the Advaitic union or *nirvikalpa samādhi* in their writings:

> When one reaches Brahman
> which is praised as the highest
> Often by Vedas and Agamas,
> sensual experiences, food, evil,
> passion, anger, cheat and threat
> will completely vanish.   (Iḍaikkāḍar, 24)

> No more do I exist
> nor does the Lord!
> There is no 'I' anymore
> So also there is no Satguru
> anymore!   (Agappēyar, 70)

It may be noted that in general the *cittars* adopt theistic terms to express the nature of their union with God. Śaivite terms abound in their writings.

In the following verses Kudambai Cittar brings out clearly the supremacy of the mystical union over knowledge, privacy, formalities, yoga, *bhakti* and worship:

Is knowledge of any use
to those whose hearts bubble with joy
while they remain
in the conscious state of bliss?   (15)

Is privacy necessary
for those who cross over death
and tread on the path
that is unique?   (13)

What's the necessity for a veil
for those who roam about
in the light in the city?   (29)

For those who are in the company
of their husband—Lord
where is the need for formalities?   (32)

Will the six circles be of any use
for the wise who have risen up
from the basic triangle?   (17)

Would the liberated one
need any singing?   (20)

For the wise who wander about
like a dead corpse—
where's the need for cymbals?   (24)

Agappēyar declares that those who have known their real
selves will not attach themselves with anything whatsoever. (24, 78)

The *cittars* speak the language of the *bhaktas* when they attempt
to describe the mystical nature of their union with the Lord. A
typical example is a lyric written by Tāyumānavar in bridal terms.
He conveys his experience in the words of a girl who narrates her
intimate union with her lover to a friend of hers:

The beginningless One,
Yet who is the beginning of all,
Who is light divine
appeared to me as speechless one

and spoke to me, my sister,
with words unspoken!
    He is Śaṅkara, the self-existing One!

How shall I narrate the words he spoke!
Cunningly he made me sit alone
and with no aid
he made me enjoy the state of bliss!
My sister, he did embrace me!
    He is Śaṅkara, the self-existing One!

He asked me to give up all attachments
and cling to him alone!
How shall I narrate to you, my sister
the joy, I obtained in his embrace?
    He is Śaṅkara, the self-existing One!

I was educated, my sister!
If I say this in open, I will spoil my career!
But, you see, he is not my illegal lover!
He is my Lord who keeps me
Under his own care
    He is Śaṅkara, the self-existing One!

54—Ānanda Kaḷippu

The *cittars* often refer to their mystical experience in terms of *transcendental space.*

Pattiragiriyār speaks of the state as the 'one great open space' (éka veḷi, 96). He also refers to it as 'the great space beyond the six *ādārams* and supreme space' (*paraveḷi*, 110). *Sivavākkiyar* also calls it 'the space of broad day light' (*veṭṭaveḷi*), Iḍaikkāḍar uses the expression *veṭṭaveḷināḍu* (the country of broad day light, 88). Pāmbāṭṭiyār combines Vedānta with the transcendental space, (*vedāntaveḷi*). The *cittars* connect Brahman or Para Śivam or Sadā-Śivam with the transcendental space. This terminology has yogic affiliations also. It is particularly connected with the yogic concept of transcending the top of the head through the thousand petalled circle (*Sahasrāram*). Tirumūlar speaks of this as 'the upper opening' (602) and equates it with 'the supreme space' (*paraveḷi*, 591). The yogi who has raised his *kuṇḍalinī* fire from *mūlādhāram* through the central *nāḍī* with controlling of breath and sends it out through the opening on top of his head is called the Yogi who has attained the first rank—(*Talaippu eida Yōgi*) (Tirumūlar, 732).

The transcendental space is also called pāḻ (vacuuity) by some *cittars*. Tirumūlar refers to it as the vacuuity to be found in the transcendental space of grace (*aruḷveḷippāḻ*). It is to be recognized over against vacuuity of *māyā* (*māyappaḻ*) and vacuuity of *jīva*. (*jīvappaḻ*), (Tirumūlar 2457). The three vacuuities are often referred to together as 'the three vacuuities' (*muppāḻ*) Paṭṭinattār Iḍaikkāḍar and Agappeyar make reference to pāḻ in their writings.

The transcendental space is also spoken of in terms of light. Tirumūlar calls it *Sōttiveḷi* (the space of light) (2766). It is the space of Śiva (2761). This resplendent divine light (*akaṇḍa veḷi*) is presented as the most brilliant over against the cosmic light or the light of Sun (*aṇḍaoḷi*) and the light of *jīva* (*piṇḍaoḷi*). Although *jīvas* have the divine light within themselves they are marred by the light of the Sun (Tirumūlar, 2761).

The *cittars* describe the indescribable nature of this state where God is seen as open space, vacuuity or light resplendent. The supreme experience of God, according to them, is beyond description. It transcends all human knowledge. The only means available to express it is silence. The only possible state discovered to retain the experience is the state of conscious sleep or the state akin to the condition of the dead body.

Tirumūlar considers this state of speechlessness as the supreme state which transcends the six ends (*ṣaḍāndam*) of Śaiva Siddhānta philosophy. They are *nādāndam, podāndam, yōgandam, védāndam, kalāndam* and *cittāndam*.

Pāmbāṭṭiyār proclaims:

> Do not utter words
> my dear snake!
> Be quiet and dance
> so that,
> Our reaching of the supreme state
> may be made known.   (122)

> Those who have seen the truth
> Will not describe it.
> Those who give descriptions of it
> will never experience it!   (105)

Pattiragiriyār sings extensively about this state and expresses his longing for attaining the same:

> When shall I reach the state
> of perfect speechlessness
> forgetting rituals and ceremonies
> performed in love?   (152)

He compares the state to the speechlessness of a dumb person who had a dream but could not narrate the experience in words. He longs to attain that stage:

> When shall I know the state of bliss
> which is indescribable
> as the dream of a dumb person?   (182)

He equates the state with a kind of conscious sleep. His long poem of lamentation opens with the following verse:

> When shall I attain bliss
> with the state of conscious sleep
> with my ego suppressed
> and my senses destroyed?   (1)

His further description of the state includes equating the same with the state of a child, wandering ghost and corpse:

> Oh for the day I become child-like,
> wander about as deaf and dumb,
> and live like a departed spirit
> with great love for you! (my Lord).   (17)

> Oh for the day I attain the state
> in which I'll be free
> from birth and death
> and become speechless and breathless
> with no thought and forgetfulness
> and be just dead.   (124)

Paṭṭiṇattār also speaks about the ghost-like wandering of the liberated persons:

> Wandering like departed spirits,
> the men of true wisdom
> lay themselves down like corpses.
> Like stray dogs they eat
> what is given as alms.
> Their movements are like
> those of foxes.
> They treat all women
> as their own mother
> and teach simplicity to all.
> Like little children indeed
> they live their lives.   (122)

The Pāśupatas, a group of sectarian Śaivites practised this kind of wandering and conscious sleep. According to *Pāśupata Sūtra*, "the adept in this stage should wander like a *preta* (ghost); should smear his body with ashes and dust like a poor man or a lunatic; should not cut his hair, beard or nails; should pretend to sleep while awake; should tremble as if sick; should limp; should make amorous gestures at women; and should speak non-sense".[1]

It appears that some *cittars*, like Paṭṭinattār were influenced by the teachings of the Pāśupata School.

Tirumūlar states that in the states of conscious or mystical sleep the Śiva-yogis see within themselves *Śivalōka*, *Śivayoga* and *Śivabhōga*.

> By the yogic conscious sleep
> they have seen within themselves
> *Śivalōkam, Śivayōgam* and *Sivabhōgam*.
> How shall I explain the bliss of those
> who have seen all these three
> in the state of conscious sleep?   (173)

Some *cittars* describe the mystical state as *Samarasam* (*Samarasa*). The meaning of the phrase is variously stated as 'equality'

----

1 *Pāśupata Sūtra*, 3, 11-17. Quoted in David Kingsley, Through the Looking Glass, *History of Religion* (HOR), Vol. 13, p. 294.

'harmony', 'identity' and 'impartiality' (colloquial).[1] Maraimalai
Adigal has emphasised the harmonizing element in *Samarasam*.
According to him it functions towards "a harmonizing of all men
by pointing to a common truth to which all could subscribe".[2]
Isaac Thambiah has pointed out that *Samarasam* should not be
mistaken for "a colourless eclectism, an anaemic acquiescence in
the pacific thought that all religions are the same".[3] This phrase
has been used by *cittars* like Tāyumānavar with specific reference
to the harmony between Vedānta and Siddhānta. As Thambiah
observes this harmony is spoken particularly in the matter of
relationship of the soul to God. Speaking about Tāyumānavar's
teachings he says that "in the postulate that God and the soul
'are not one, nor yet two', the two teachings, Vedāntic and Sid-
dhāntic are brought into unison, *samarasam*".[3] The poet expressly
speaks of 'the Godly *samarasa* bliss which consists in an affirma-
tion of neither oneness nor twoness'.[4]

Tāyumānavar calls this state of awareness as "the bliss in which
one does not say what it is (the relation between soul and God).
It is neither oneness nor twoness.

Tambiah has quoted passages from P. Muthia Pillai and J.M.
Nallaswami Pillai, to show the different standpoints of the two
Śaivite scholars with regard to the meaning of *samarasam*. Muthia
Pillai is said to have stated that *samarasam* is in fact the acknow-
ledgement of the complementary nature of Vedānta and Siddhānta. J.M. Nallaswami Pillai prefers the meaning 'impartiality'.
He contends that there will be differences of outlook in the six
creeds while the *samarasa* mind recognizes the good that is in
each and views all with non-contentions, uncertain 'impartiality'.
With regard to Vedānta and Siddhānta he would notice the *samarasam* in retaining of their distinctness of the two systems of
thought. He quotes Tirumūlar's lines "Vedānta which says that
(the soul) becomes (god) and the Siddhānta which says that (the
soul) is distinct..." to support his view.

The observations of all the three scholars are helpful to understand the deeper meaning of the phrase *samarasam* and the possible

---

1   Madras University Tamil Lexicon, Vol. III.
2   Maraimalai Adigal, *Śaiva Siddhānta Jñānabōdham*, p. 65.
3   Isaac Thambiah, *Hymns of a Śaiva Saint*, London; p. xxxl.
4   *Op. cit.*, p. xxxi.

ways of its application to the systems of thought. *Samarasam* does point out the fact that there are certain things common to the different systems of thought. The comparable elements do not however point in the direction of complete identity. They maintain their distinct characteristics at all costs and thus provide clues to a deeper undertsanding of their relationship which can be best understood in terms of 'complementation' and 'impartiality'.

It is to be noted that Tirumūlar and Tāyumānavar speak of *samarasam* not at the expense of Śaivism but with firm grounding in its basic tenets.

Tirumūlar declares that he who adheres to Vedānta and Siddhānta which reveal *Śiva* in the supreme space of grace and the soul in its surpassed state as the dancing hall of Śiva, will obtain *Śivajñānam*, (2356).

Tāyumānavar does speak of the *cittars* as those who have known the *samarasam* of Vedānta and Siddhānta. He also refers to their pure mystical experience as the *'advaita* union' (293). He also describes them as those who have established themselves in *Śivayoga*. He is faithful to his Śaivite convictions. He declares the supremacy of Śaivism and its distinctiveness in a famous verse:

> Śaivism is the real path indeed.
> It reveals to you in the Hall Divine
> the eternal reality
> which is beyond the reach
> of all other schools of thought
> and makes you attain the same.
> Don't you forsake this
> and run after religions
> which are false.
> O people of the world,
> Come to join us
> so that you will have the vision
> of the hall divine.   30—*Kāḍum karaiyum*

Closely related with the concept of *samarasam* is *sanmārgam* (the true path) in Tamil Śaivism. It is the highest of the four *mārgas* spoken in Śaiva Siddhānta. Tirumūlar upholds this path and declares it as the divine Śaivite path (1451). He brings out the Śaivite implications of the phrase to the full when he states that *sanmārgam* is becoming one with Śiva, after one disassociates himself completely with the three malas...Those who have obtained this state will enjoy *Śivajñāna* (1454). He calls *sanmārgam* by the name *taṛcivatattuvam* (knowing Śiva as he is in himself') (1450).

Speaking about the *Sanmārgīs* he says that they are divine (1455) and they triumph over death (1450).

Voice against Religious Bigotry

The Siddhas were the first ones to raise their voice against various kinds of social injustice prevailing in society with religious sanction. Several of the Tamil Siddhas condemn casteism and Brāhmaṇism. Although they were radical and outspoken in their social attitude, they cannot be considered as social revolutionaries in the real sense of the term. Kamil Zvelebil points out that they did not aim at "the radical structural change of the Hindu society and some of them dreamed of a future when there would be no castes."[1] Pattiragiriār for instance laments: "Oh! for the day when we shall live without divisions of caste, according to the teachings of the First Kabilar" (125). Śivavākkiyar strongly condemns caste distinction and untouchability by plainly affirming "that there is no difference between an outcaste and a Brahmin woman in flesh, skin or bones and that this may be experimented by simply sleeping with both of them" (38). Śivavākkiyar is very critical of temple worship and seriously questions the sanctity and venerability of the idols installed therein. He cries:

> After all, what are these temples
> and the sacred tanks?
> Tell me you poor slave
> who worship in temples and tanks!
> Temples are in the mind
> and so also the tanks......   (33)

Why do you utter mantras

---

1. *Op. cit.*, p. 69.

murmuring and whispering?
Why do you go round the
erected stone
treating it as God
and adorn it with garlands of flowers?
I pity you!
Will the fixed stone speak
even when the Lord could dwell within?
Will the cooking vessel
know the taste of
the curry cooked in it?　　　　　　　　　　(496)

It is not correct to describe the Siddhas as a category of free thinkers with yogic capacities over against the *bhaktas,* who were emotional and adapted themselves to the cultic pattern of temple worship. In fact both yoga and *bhakti* are integrated in the lives and teachings of several Siddhas like Paṭṭinattār. I quote a stanza from Śivavākkiyar to illustrate this truth:

You will never find the Lord
in the pages of the four Vedas.
Nor in the study of these scriptures
nor by chanting of the *mantras.*
Melt with your heart inside only...
and announce the Truth......　　　　　　　　(36)

The Siddhas have made their own contribution towards the understanding of *mukti* by the concepts of imperishable body and glorious life without death.

The Tamil Siddhas deserve commendation for the courage with which they fought out religious bigotry of their times and for paving the way for a counter-tradition with strong anti-cultic and anti-Brāhmaṇic elements. A.V. Subramania Aiyer commends them "for their heroism and strength of convictions".[1]

It will not be out of place here to state that Tamil Śaivism itself is claimed to be Siddha Mārga. Tiru Vi. Ka. the great Śaivite Tamil scholar, is of the opinion that Siddha Mārga or the spiritual

---

1 *Op. cit.,* p. 82.

view of the universe held by the Siddhas had spread and prevailed among all the peoples of the world.

The sacred *Tevāram* which contains the mystical writings of Appar, Sundarar and Sambandar speaks of persons who have adopted the spiritual or religious path in life, broadly into two classes. Those who are striving to see God are *bhaktas*, while those who have already had the supreme privilege of seeing God and obtaining illumination of soul are *Siddhas*. All the Siddhas are alike in their spiritual experience and divine wisdom; but each has his own way of giving expression to his spiritual quest. This is the reason why the Siddhas rise above all religious barriers. Their poetry breathes the spirit of universal love and brotherhood and pleads for an ethical life completely free from sectarian limitations.[1]

It is claimed by Tiru Vi. Ka. and others that great Śaivite Saints, namely Appar, Sundarar, Sambandar and Māṇikkavāsagar, who lived between the 6th and 9th centuries, have among other things revived the Siddha Mārga which was declining in the Tamil country. All the four saints have joyfully declared that they were liberated from death and the chain of births by the Lord Śiva. According to Śaivite tradition and sacred records, these four saints did not die but passed on into direct communion with God and attained deathless life and eternal bliss.

THE SIDDHA MĀRGA OF RAMALINGA SWAMY

Ramalinga's contributions to the tradition of the Tamil *cittars* may be classified under the two broad headings of Religious Experience and Religious Life. The main sources for the teachings of Ramalinga are his numerous poems and pamphlets, together with his treatise on *Jīvakāruṇyam*. A few of the sayings and conversations of Ramalinga recorded by his biographers are also helpful in reconstructing his message.

RELIGIOUS EXPERIENCE

Songs of Divine Grace

Ramalinga's *Tiruvaruptā* consisting of well over five thousand and eight hundred verses provides us ample material to deduce his

---

1   For further details see T.P. Meenashisundaram's article on *Cittars* in *Kalaikkalanjiam* (Tamil Encyclopaedia), Madras University, Vol. IV, 1982.

spiritual biography. The book is divided into six *tirumurais* or sections which are full of *bhakti* poems and lyrics. These were sung by Ramalinga for a period of about thirty-nine years. The first four *tirumurais* consisting of 3028 verses were written during his early life in Madras. This period would extend upto 1858. The fifth *tirumurai* consisting of 237 verses was composed between 1858 and 1867. This was the period he resided in Karunkuḷi. Upto this period he was attached to cultic worship and visited several temples including the famous one in Chidambaram. The sixth *tirumurai* consisting of 2551 poems was written during the last seven years of his life (1867-74). It is the most remarkable period in his life. During this period Ramalinga was preoccupied with thoughts relating to Siddhahood. He claims to have attained the same in several verses. While making bold proclamations about his exaltation to Siddhahood he offers his invitation to all to join him in this new experience of his. The impact of some of the leading *cittars* like Tirumūlar and Tāyumānavar is discernible in his writings of this period. He had contacts with some of the Sādhus and *cittars* of his day and it is quite possible that he widened his knowledge of Siddhahood and deepened his interest in attaining the same through the contacts with the Sādhus. The Siddhic material in this *tirumurai* is mixed with the traditional *bhakti* modes of praise, adoration and confession.

Ramalinga did not allow his disciples to publish the sixth *tirumurai* during his life time. He thought that the time was not ripe yet. Only the first four *tirumurais* were published during his life time in 1867. The fifth was published in 1880 and the sixth in 1885. However, the sixth *tirumurai* material might have been read by some of Ramalinga's intimate disciples during his life time. It is interesting to note that Toḷuvūr Velayutam, Ramalinga's most intimate disciple who had first undertook the publication of *Tiruvaruṭpā* did not ever publish the sixth *tirumurai*. As in the case of many other *cittars,* Ramalinga's writings became more popular and widely read only after his life time. It is difficult to arrange the poems of the sixth *tirumurai* in their chronological order. An attempt, however, is made by Ooranadigaḷ in his latest edition of *Tiruvaruṭpā*.

A Bhakta and Siddha

Ramalinga is keen on maintaining his position both as *bhakta* and Siddha. He tries to show the close connection between *bhakti* and *siddhi* in the poems of the sixth *tirumurai*. He seeks to maintain a balance between the two. He shows remarkable talent as a devotional poet in putting the *siddhi* ideas and concepts in *bhakti* poems. He is thoroughly convinced that he comes in the line of both the Śaivite poets and the *cittars*. He believes that his Lord has granted him a unique place in the galaxy of the Śaivite saints as well as the *cittars*. This prominent position of his is stated clearly in the following two verses:

> ...You placed me my Lord
> at the very centre
> in the assembly of your saints—
> the Śaivites!
> As a deity indeed am treated by you
> who dance in the Hall of Wisdom.   (4800)

> ...You placed me my Lord
> at the very centre
> of the holy band of your servants—
> the *cittars*!
> In the form of wisdom indeed
> am brought up by you
> while you dance in the Hall.   (4801)

Ramalinga is keen on pointing out the mutual interdependence of *bhakti* and *siddhi*. While accepting *siddhi* to be the ultimate goal for spiritual maturity he is never tired of proclaiming that *bhakti* is the sole means for attaining *siddhi*:

> People of the world,
> focus your thoughts on the Lord
> who is self-existent
> who is all-pervading
> yet different from all—
> the Unique Lord!
> He is father and mother to me,

He is meditated and praised
by his beloved saints
as the Supreme, the very seed of the Supreme
as the very life of the seed;
who is choice ambrosia tasting sweet
like sugar mixed with honey.
If you do so,
You will obtain the superb *siddhi*
of living for ages...   (5589)

Siddhahood according to Ramalinga is not something that is
sought for performing miracles. He would rather live the life of a
bhakta and live it to the full.

I desire not to die
nor to continue this life
nor even to be born anymore.
I desire not popularity
to be known as great!
Nor do I desire to perform
any miracle to my credit   (3400)

... I take delight, my Lord,
in watching your dance
in the Hall of Wisdom
as well as in the Golden Hall,
in singing and dancing daily
and in making happy
the living beings of this world   (3401)

These statements are comparable with a verse of Tirumular
which says that the divine light unobtainable by *cittars* had made
itself accessible to the *bhaktas* and granted them *mukti*.   (271)

The bestowal of Siddhahood on him

The bestowal of Siddhahood on him is interpreted by Ramalinga as the answer to his prayer for the same to be put in the
service of others. In a verse he narrates the words of the Lord
spoken to him thus:

...It was your wish to remove all evils
and pave the path of goodness
and enable all attain
true and happy life.
May it be according to your wish
May you exhibit *Siddhis.*
We have made you the dispenser
of the gracious light,
We will never forsake you.

(3676)

Apart from *bhakti* he also connects *mukti* and *buddhi* (knowledge) with *siddhi* and seeks to harmonize them all in the life of a *bhakta-siddha.* Speaking about *mukti* he observes it to be the penultimate state which precedes *siddhi* which is the attainment of that final state (4615, 248). The tension that normally exists between *buddhi* and *siddhi* is portrayed in a verse thus:

When I went to see
the divine dance in the Hall
The girl *siddhi*
caught hold of me by hand!
Will *buddhi,* the girl who is already mine
be pleased at it?
or will she stop loving me
and depart me with anger?
will they both get along nicely
or will they quarrel with each other?
will they bring forth children for me?
what your holy will about this
is not clear to me, my Lord!

(338)

Direct Experience of God

Like the other *cittars,* Ramalinga is much interested in speaking about his first hand experience of God. He adopts various forms of expression to communicate his inner experience. He follows the patterns set by his predecessors. His poems reveal his familiarity with the *bhakti* as well as the *siddhi* literature. Like Paṭṭinattār and Tāyumānavar he combines the style and diction of the *bhakti* poets and the *siddhas.* It may be stated tha the distinguished himself as a *siddha* among the *bhaktas* and a *bhakta* among the *siddhas*. While narrating his intimate spiritual experiences as a *siddha* he appends them with praises and petitions which abound in the writings of *bhakti* poets. The following verse from his poem *tiruvaruṭpēru* (The Gift of Grace Divine) is a fine illustration for such blending:

> You made me ascend through the staircase
> and reach the city where the supreme dance takes place;
> You showed me the temple at the centre of the city
> and at the threshold of the temple tower
> You opened the sacred door for me
> but closed it before I could enter.
>
> I beseech you to open the door again.
> This is the opportune moment.
> I cannot wait anymore.
> Hasten my Lord—the dancer at the Hall
> to bestow your grace on me.   (3780)

The first part of the verse speaks of the yogic ascension of the *siddha*. Although the yogic process is not stated elaborately with the conventional terms, it is implied in this part of the verse. The latter part is the cry of a *bhakta* who longs for the experience once again. He requests that the vision may be granted to him again together with the bestowal of divine grace.

Similar cries of aspirations are to be found in the following lines as well:

> You gave me the key to open
> the chest containing great riches.
> I now try to open and take the treasure.
> Do not deceive me.
> Hasten to bestow your grace.   (3781)
>
> You gave me a helping hand
> and lifted me up.
> You gave me legs
> for my enjoyment of the wide world.
> Now you should give me

the body that will not perish.
I will not leave you till you grant the same.
Now that I have ascended up
I do not like to descend anymore.   (3784)

Crossing all the woods I reached the country
and saw the beautiful sight
of the golden walls of your city!
I saw the flags on top of the forts;
they added beauty to the sight.
At the entrance of the temple
I got relieved of all infirmities
and I obtained *siddhi*
to control my mischievous sense organs.
I now sing about the Hall of Wisdom!
My Lord,
This is the opportune moment;
Fill my heart with your very self.   (3820)

Ramalinga is fond of narrating the divine vision as well as the
experience of the Lord in terms of the 'divine dance in the Hall
of Wisdom'. This vision and dance symbolize the divine activity
of the indwelling god. The Hall of Wisdom in Chidambaram
points to the 'natural bliss', 'the transcendental space' and *Śuddha
Śiva* state. Ramalinga's chief concern in life was to reach that
state wherefrom come all *Siddhis*. He sings:

God is One indeed
in the divine Hall of Wisdom
wherefrom comes the light
which gives rise to all *siddhis*.   (3270)

Pondering over God's transcendent nature or the *Śuddha Śiva
Veḷi* he pours out his heart to God:

You are beyond the seven spheres;
the Vedas cannot find your real depth.
You are in those spheres and
You absorb them all in yourself!
You are such a comprehensive sphere!—
the sphere of *Śuddha Śivam*.   (4157)

Ramalinga also refers to the highest religious experience as obtainable when one passes beyond the six *antas* of *nādānta, kalānta, bodhānta, yogānta, vedānta* and *siddhānta.* The direct experience of God beyond religion is basic to the teachings of Ramalinga. He narrates his own experience of the beyond in many verses. A poem which he has rendered in typical *cittar* style is worth our notice.

(Addressing her friend a young girl joyfully sings narrating her inner experience):

Look my dear friend!
Upon the clouds I saw
a peacock dancing!
But very soon
it changed its appearance
to a cuckoo

I stopped jumping
and started the search.
I did find the Lord!—
the bestower of grace,
the dancer in the sacred hall.

Now my friend,
I have given up caste and creed,
I have seen for myself
the light of grace!
So my friend,
I have abandoned the unreal
and as I set out
I found my Lord
who dances in the Hall.   (4947—4950)

Ramalinga uses the word *podu* 'Common' or 'public' which is one of the names given to the dancing hall of Chidambaram. He is keen on emphasising the deeper meaning of the word along the lines followed by Tirumūlar and Tāyumānavar. Tirumūlar brings out the universal aspect of *podu* and *cirrampalam* by stating that every place is Chidambaram in its own right and that the divine dance is to be seen everywhere, (2722). Tāyumānavar states

in his *citampara rakasiyam* (14.12) that people of all religions
come to worship in Chidambaram. Ramalinga during the last
seven years of his life was keen on preaching about the Lord's
dance in the form of light is to be seen in the Sabai at Vadalur.
He goes on to say that Vadalur is a better place for his dance.
One of his popular lyrics brings out the idea:

> All the songs I sing are songs
> on the dancing hall divine—
> the golden as well as the subtle one.   (5793)

The universal aspect of *podu* is linked up with the diverse mani-
festations of God stressed by Ramalinga. It is interesting to see
how in a poem written in the form of a conversation between two
girls, he brings out the point. One of them represents the *bhakta—
siddha* who is married to the Lord. She is awaiting his arrival. In
the meantime her friend asks her several questions. One of the
questions relates to the name of the husband—Lord. The reply
comes from the soul wedded to the Lord thus:

> You're asking my friend
> to tell you my husband's name,
> Now listen!
> His name is Arhat, Buddha, the Ancient,
> Indra, Nārāyana, Hara, Ādi Śiva,
> Sadā Śiva, Śakti Śivam, Param
> Brahman, Śuddha Brahman,
> Turia, Śuddha Śiva.
> All these are his siddhic manifestations!   (5801)

Ramalinga uses often the analogy of light to describe the nature
of divine grace. This concept is cherished in yogic teachings. But
Ramalinga does not elaborate the yogic process like several other
siddhas. But he does reveal his acquaintance with the yoga of
breath control practised by raising the *kuṇḍalinī* through the six
ādhāras and drinking the ambrosia or nectar. He makes reference
to the ambrosia in several verses, especially the ones arranged
under the title *Śivayogam.*

I have crossed the sea of *māyā*
and reached the shore
where the greatness of grace is found.
There I drank the sweet ambrosia   (3864)

Open the door
you who love me
with a new love!
My Śiva, the dancer king!
So that—
I may drink the nectar of the moon
and rule over the sphere of your Lordship   (3832)

'ambrosia of grace'   (3833)

'ambrosia which offers deathlessness'   (3834)

'ambrosia which gives knowledge'   (3836)

'ambrosia of the Hall of Wisdom'   (5598)

'ambrosia which is preferred to
in the Vedas as the powerful *siddhi*'   (3837)

'the sweet ambrosia which is
to be found above the seven states'   (3836)

'the clear ambrosia'   (5589)

'the sacred ambrosia at the
top of the mountain of light'   (3841)

Only once in his writings Ramalinga uses the term 'sahaja'.
In a verse included in the fifth *tirumurai* he says:

What you have done to me is a wonder.
How shall I narrate it?
You imparted knowledge to me
an ignorant lad.
You showed me the beginning and end
and several other states.
You showed me the mystery
relating to the bliss of the Siddhas
You showed me the state of deathlessness

and the state of *sahaja.*
You showed the place
where my mind got dissolved in you
and made me happy!
None has the power of your grace!   (3038)

The contrast between the direct experience of God and the
knowledge of God through the means of philosophy and religion
is brought out sharply in the writings of Ramalinga. He adopts
the metre used by *Kudambaic cittar,* in one of his poems, to con-
vey this truth.

Dialogue with the heart

To behold him who is beyond time
Why should you care for time at all?
my good heart,
Why should you?

To behold the Lord directly
no obstacle is set before you
my good heart,
none indeed.

To drink the nectar you have in your hand
why should you feel sorry at all
my good heart,
why should you?
To behold the master who transcends all *tattvas*
Why should you consider *tattvas* any more
my good heart,
why should you?
We have drunk the ambrosia well
So we will not hycough
my good heart,
we will never!   (4287-4296)

Charismatic Gifts

Ramalinga's writings in the sixth *tirumurai* abound with statements relating to certain occasions in his life when he was blessed

with special privileges and charismatic gifts. These include visions, special instructions, bestowal of honours and *siddhis*.

Visions of the Lord Śiva and miraculous encounters with him were recurring features in the life of Ramalinga even from the days he spent in Madras. Later during his early years in Karun-kuḷi he was granted a vision in Chidambaram temple while he stood weeping at the gate. He speaks of a particular encounter with his Lord in Cuddalore when he appeared to him while he was sleeping in his room. Opening the door the Lord entered the room and gave a certain thing in his hand and urged him to relieve himself of all miseries. He sings about this in a long poem now included in the fourth *tirumurai*. According to some verses in the sixth *tirumurai* he had siddhic visions more than once and was taught yoga and *siddhis* directly by the Lord.

On one evening
You did teach me yoga
in one *nāḻikai*[1]
and granted me
the fruits of yoga
the next morning.   (4993)

While I slept one day on ground
exhausted in body and confused in mind
pondering your grace
and forgetting the world
and all its affairs,
you, my guru, came near me at day break
and woke my up.

Addressing me as 'son' you said:
'It is not good that you perish
without following the paths of yoga or *Jñāna*—
So get up! Work them out!
Drink the ambrosia of grace'.   (3674)

From the above two verses it becomes clear that he developed the desire for yoga and at a particular stage realized for certain that he was a yogi taught and approved by the Lord himself.

---

1 Minute.

Another vision of his is to the effect of the Lord merging into him.

> One night
> You, my guru, appeared to me
> in your form of wisdom.
> Embracing me you entered into me.
> Relieving me of all misery
> You are now seated firmly in my heart.　　　　(3675)

In another verse he connects an earlier vision at Chidambaram with a fresh one he had in Vadalur and speaks of further bestowal of grace.

> I stood in a corner on that day
> at the entrance of the sacred hall
> pondering on your grace.
> Remembering the gracious words
> you spoke to me on that occasion
> I waited for the blessed day
> and spent many days in expectation.
> And today,
> as soon as I told you
> 'this day would be auspicious
> to show your grace to me'
> you bestowed the same on me.
> Great indeed is your love in this world!　　　　(4756)

Ramalinga states that he was taught everything in a moment by the Lord who places his feet on his head (4182) and that his soft nature of fear and worries of sorrow is transformed into a bold and happy state (4985).

According to tradition most of the Tamil *cittars* were encountered by the Lord in the form of a guru and they were initiated into yoga. But they do not say much about that experience in their writings. Ramalinga is following the example of Tāyumānavar who constantly mentions and praises the *mouna guru* who imparted divine knowledge to him. Ramalinga says that he sees visions in his heart.

I have given up all evil
and drank your ever flooding grace.
I see visions in my heart—
Visions I have never seen before...   (3892)

Ramalinga proclaims that the rare visions granted to him and
the special grace bestowed on him by the Lord have raised him
to the status of a divine being by virtue of which state he was
made to be the Lord's emissary on the earth uttering the very
words of the Lord. Speaking about the attainment of divinity
Ramalinga says:

You made me my Lord
ascend to heights unthinkable,
endowed me with powers divine
and shown me blessed visions
hitherto kept unrevealed.
You are indeed the supreme dancer
and the crown-head of all Siddhas.   (4763)

Ramalinga affirms that *siddhi* is a divine quality and it is directly
received from Śiva whom he calls 'the crown head of all siddhas'.
He believes in divine commission received by the siddhas and
particularly in his case:

You my guru made me fit
with the bestowal of grace on me;
by commissioning me with your own word
to perform all *siddhis*.   (3665)

"Since
the evil path made up of
manifold religions and sects
has extended itself so far,
those who do not know the true path
had gone into absolute darkness
having died many a time.
So discard the evil path.
and build the path of *Sanmārga*
which bestows the divine ambrosia
of the path open to all."

> Thus you spoke to me, O Naṭarāja,
> my master and king.   (3696)

This leads him to proclaim that the father-son relationship is maintained between the Lord and himself. He claims himself to be the dearest son of the Lord:

> I am the son of the Gracious Siddha
> who is praised by all the liberated Ones.   (5593)

Speaking to the Lord he says, "you made me your pet child" (3895; 4057). He states that his adoption to divine sonship is preceded by his drinking of the ambrosia (4059-61). Ramalinga as the dearest and unique son of the Lord endeavours to establish that his message is literally the message coming from the Lord. In a verse written at a time when his message was not accepted at large he says:

> My friends,
> It is my firm belief that
> the words I speak are in fact
> the words of the Lord.
> This is the opportune time
> to meet the Lord who is to come—
> the divine dancer—
> and attain gifts he bestows
> graciously.
> The Sacred Hall dancer
> has become my own self;
> He is not 'he' anymore,
> nor am I 'I' any longer.
> The words I speak are
> the words of my Lord who speaks through me.
> They are not my own!   (5502, 5503)

He makes his sonship to be attested by the words of his Lord when he says in a verse that the Lord had confirmed the truth thus:

> The words you speak my son

for correcting the people of this world
are of course my words!   (3679)

His unique status is further described by him as being an all-powerful siddha with divine commission to do the five great divine deeds of creation, protection, dissolution, *tirodhānam* (hiding) and *anugraham* (bestowal of grace).

In 18 verses he states that the Lord has entirely left at his disposal the five divine deeds or commissioned him to perform the acts. (3948, 4045)

Ramalinga claims that he attained the gift of making gold. His first disciple Toluvur Velayatam in his testimony to the Theosophical Society has stated that Ramalinga was a great alchemist. Ramalinga speaks of his achievement in alchemy of transforming baser metal into gold in only one verse. He is specific in stating that this was a gift and it was taught by the Lord.

...You taught me the means
of making gold
and came to reside in my heart...   (3962)

In his correspondence with Ratna Mudaliar, Ramalinga asks him to send him testing stones of gold and silver together with a scale, and also acknowledges the receipt of the same. He writes in the letter that the matter should be kept secret.

The *Siddhi* par excellence achieved by Ramalinga is *Kāya-siddhi* according to the hundreds of references made in the sixth *tirumurai*. A number of verses are written requesting the Lord to bestow on him the *siddhi* of deathlessness or obtaining *mukti* along with the body. These verses are scattered all along in the sixth *tirumurai* and it is difficult to see them in the chronological order as there is no internal evidence to mark clearly the stages of the spiritual life. Ramalinga declares in many verses that he has obtained the *śuddha, praṇava* and *jñāna* bodies. He sings:

You my great gracious Light have given me the power
to obtain the three types of bodies.   (*Akaval*, 237-8)

He also calls the *śuddha deha, svarṇa deha* and body of life.

I have got my body

which is affected by age
changed into a golden body.   (4096)

Truly I have obtained the golden body.   (4832)

I have learnt the culture of *cirrampalam*
and have obtained the body of light...   (4833)

My Lord the divine dancer
entered into me
and bestowed upon me
the true light which is his grace
and lifted me up.
He has changed my body
to the present resplendent state!
How shall I narrate this in words?   (3863)

The three bodies are together referred to as imperishable or
eternal bodies. Ramalinga states in many verses that the *mukti*
obtained by him is nothing less than that.

You granted me the body
which will by no means be destroyed.   (3867)

I have obtained
the imperishable and divine form.   (3896)

Tāyumānavar has sung in praise of the siddhas who have obtained the threefold *siddhi* of having transformed their bodies
into the three states of *śuddha, praṇava* and *jñāna*:

So many indeed are those
who have obtained *mukti*
with the threefold *Siddhis*.   (*Parāparakkaṇṇi* 209)

According to Ramalinga the attainment of *Śuddha deha* gives
the form of light; and *praṇava deha* gives the form of sound, the
deha of *jñāna* gives celestial form or form of grace. Sundarar is
said to have achieved the *śuddha deha* while Sambandar, Appar
and Paṭṭinattār are said to have achieved the *praṇava deha*.
Maṇikkavāsagar and Ramalinga are said to have obtained the
jñāna deha.

While narrating his experience of achieving the siddhic body of the highest order Ramalinga says that in answer to his request the Lord has transformed his sinful body into the form of bliss (3854), nature (3855), grace (56) and Śiva (3861).

This achievement is otherwise spoken as victory over death or deathlessness:

> The great gracious Light
> bestowed on me
> the boon of deathlessness.
> The great gracious Light
> said to me
> we have given you the deathless life   (209-10)

> I have seen the father
> and have attained   (4903)
> the gift of deathlessness!

> ...I am bestowed with
> the gift of deathlessness
> and I have got over
> the fear of death.   (4731)

> I asked for a body
> that could not be destroyed
> by wind or earth or air
> by fire or water of luminaries
> by death, or disease or weapons
> by planets or other evil influences
> or by any other means
> He granted the same immediately!...   (5450)

Ramalinga is not merely satisfied with the *deha śuddhi* he has obtained. He is persuading the people to obtain the same:

> You people have not known the Light Eternal
> since you did not make any effort at it.
> You have not found the ways and means
> to stop death and birth either...
> Closing your eyes you move about
> and offer nothing to those

who beg in your streets,
You mad people of the world!
Do you profit anything in your lives?   (5558)

He stresses the importance of *bhakti* as the means for attaining *kāya siddhi:*

Come you people of the world!
Let us together praise him saying,
'You are our beloved Lord, the dancer king divine
and the sweet ambrosia of grace!'
With constant thought and abounding emotion
With melted hearts filled to the brim with love
let us wet our bodies with spring like tears.
Then we shall live the glorious life without death.
Listen! I do not exaggerate anything;
nor do I tell lie. I speak the truth.
This is the opportune time for you
to enter the golden hall
as well as the subtle hall of wisdom.   (5376)

Ramalinga says that his new and modified path of *Śuddha Samarasa Sanmārgam* is the path that destroys death. The *Sanmārgī* for him is the one who does not taste death. Only *Sanmārgīs* are entitled to attain the state of deathlessness.

If you postpone your days
to learn the truth,
death the great enemy will arrive!
You can't prevent its coming.
Excepting the *Sanmārga Sangamites*
none in all the world can come forward boldly
to drive death away.
You people of the world,
listen to my words which are true.
Give up completely
the things which you are attached to now.
Cling to the divine hall of dance with love.
Then you will never taste death.   (5599)

When you see the bodies of the dead
taken to be disposed
you lament and cry aloud!
But you, people of the world,
why can't you attain
the great gift of deathlessness?
You have completely forgotten this.
Are you happy with
disease and old age?
The gentle ones will shudder at this thought.
The great path of *Sanmārga* alone
will keep away disease, old age and death.
Do understand this and come hither friends!
You will attain in no time
eternal life here and now.
True happiness will be yours indeed.   (5600)

Ramalinga would not tolerate dead bodies cremated. He believed in raising of the dead bodies back to life. Strangely enough he speaks of the resurrection of the body and 'the coming of the Lord'. He seems to have borrowed these concepts from Christianity and Islam. Ooranaḍigaḷ acknowledges the fact that these ideas are new to the Śaivite as well as the Siddhi traditions. Ramalinga's arguments against the practice of burning the dead are interesting although not convincing:

Do not Cremate

When the child is born
you bathe it
and bring it up with utmost care.
But when someone dies
you cremate the corpse.
You are devilish!
How did you consent
to take to this practice?
You put fire on those
who slept in the night
and forgot to get up in the morning.
What 'powerful'(!) people you are!

> You are only worthy to be praised
> as people whose hearts are hard
> as 'precious diamond'(!) rocks!
> Why were you born
> and why do you move about
> calling yourselves
> 'human beings'!   (5608)

It is crime to cremate

> This body of ours is God given.
> It is a crime
> to cremate the same.
> Although I warn you
> you continue to cremate.
> The blessed day is at hand
> When the Siddha-Lord
> will raise all who are dead.
> Won't you understand this
> and see the reason why
> the good people always buried their dead?
> You are like cows that are blind!   (5608)

Ramalinga proclaims in his *akaval* that the *siddhis* bestowed upon him include *karma, yoga* and *jñāna siddhis* (239-246). *Karma siddhi* according to a recorded teaching of his includes the *aṣṭamācittigaḷ* (the eight great *siddhis*) and raising the dead body before it is buried. *Yoga siddhi* makes the siddha a *parāparamārgī* with powers to raise the burnt corpse before its decaying state. When a siddha obtains the *jñāna siddhis* he is able to have at his disposal the sixty-four thousand *śaktis* and 686 crores of *mahā siddhis*. He passes beyond time and is marked with the highest kind of *siddhis* which are called the *śuddha karma, śuddha yoga* and *śuddha jñāna siddhis*.

Ramalinga makes his request for the boon of raising the dead in a number of verses. In a verse he makes the request thus:

> ...I should raise the dead and make them the servants of holy
>   Sabai;

...I also request for the state being one with you
my father with the imperishable body.　　　　(4082)

He also states in a number of places in the sixth *tirumurai* that he is given the divine gift of raising the dead to life. He is convinced that deathlessness and raising the dead go together. Only those who have attained *kāya siddhi* can raise the dead. The great Śaivite Saints Appar, Sambandar and Sundarar are said to have raised the dead on certain occasions in their lives. Ramalinga emphatically affirms in a verse that as a result of his austerities he has obtained the double gifts of deathlessness and the power to raise the dead. He adds that he is completely satisfied with his achievements and longs for nothing:

I am bestowed with two gifts,
namely the *jñāna* fulfilment
of bringing back to life
those who are dead in this world...
and the gift of deathlessness
to live in prosperity for ages.
I have given up the fear of death
I am satisfied with my present state.
I am rewarded for my austerities.　　　　(4731)

In a few verses he emphasises that raising the dead is an eschatological phenomenon which is linked up with the coming of the Lord. The following verse is worth noting. He speaks to his doubting and perturbed mind by way of confirming the hope he cherished in his heart:

Do not be afraid my heart!
This is the time for the Father to come.
Do not doubt it anymore.
Keep on proclaiming this truth to the people of the world.
Your words will not become null and go void
I swear on my God.
It is certain that we will raise the dead
rejoicing in the state of the great gracious form of light
while being praised by all the inhabitants

of this world, the heaven and the beyond!
Do not be afraid my heart!   (4875)

In another verse he states that it will be the Father, who on his
coming to the world, will raise the dead rather than himself.

Reach this place quickly
you people of the world.
The invitation I make is true indeed;
don't take that to be a false one.
This is the opportune time
for the all-powerful Siddha-Lord to come
to exhibit his great powers
by making the aged renew their youth
and by raising the dead to life.
If you accept the invitation
You will be much benefited.   (5583)

It is stated in another verse that "the Lord is coming today and
he would be seated in the place where I am; within two and half
years he will be absorbed into my body. You will know this after
two and half years"   (5818).

He prescribes the way of *bhakti* again as the means of preparing
to meet the Lord in the same verse thus:

So,
with hearts melting in love
eyes filled with rolling tears
meditate on the Lord, the gracious divine dancer,
experiencing the joyful state of ecstacy.   (5583)

He also states that the coming of the Lord will be the time for him
to be fed with nectar and the occasion to see visions which he
had not been granted thus for.

Do come here, you people of earth.
Know that this is the time
for my father to come!
the time for him to feed me with churned nectar
of superior quality—
the time to show me

the vision hitherto not shown.
Don't you roam about unwittingly.
You can certainly obtain the joy
that is mine now.
I do not treat you as different
from my own self.
Get up and realize your good selves.
Do not stay any more
in the broken cistern of religion!...　　　　　　　　　(5586)

Ramalinga's contributions to Tamil Siddhic thoughts include in particular his eschatological statements about the coming of the Father and the subsequent raising of the dead. Ooranaḍigaḷ acknowledges that these are ideas new to Tamil Siddhic or Śaivite traditions. It is quite possible that Ramalinga had come into contact with the teachings of Christianity and Islam and borrowed these concepts from those faiths. In all his endeavours to foster the Tamil Siddhic tradition he is keen on stating his unique position and achievements. Although his claims regarding the achievement of the *siddhi* to raise the dead were not put into print during his life time, people from nearby and far off places have come to know about his fame as a siddha and yogi and approached him with requests of healing and raising their dead back to life. Ramalinga obviously never raised the dead during his life time. Maraimalai Adigal records in his diary, written in 1910 that when he visited Vadalur, he came to know through reliable sources that Ramalinga never performed miracles. In one of the pamphlets the Swamy released in an uncontrollable situation, he made his position clear:

> We are not sure whether a miracle is going to take place or not; nor can we be sure of its happening now or at some other time in the future. So be on your guard and do not be deceived.

Spirituality According to Ramalinga

Like many other Tamil *cittars* Ramalinga denounces the cultic practices. Although he is not anti-cultic to the core, he stresses the importance of puritanic religion against the cultic. He would not completely break away from cultic worship as did many other *cittars.* He is chiefly concerned in popularising his conviction that the Lord's dancing place is not confined exclusively to Chidambaram. This he does by stating the equal importance of Vadalur or even by showing that the *jñāna sabai* that he has built at Vadalur transcends the other cultic places of worship. He has taken seriously the aspects of God as Light and God as Love and has set up the pattern of worshipping God in the form of light. He was, at an earlier stage, i.e., before setting up the *sabai*, keen on emphasizing the importance of idol worship. He participated in discussion with Seethara Naickar, a Brahmo Samajist on the subject of idol worship in Cuddalore. According to the recorded statements of his disciples, cited by Ooranaḍigaḷ, he won the debate. There seems to be another version of the event. This is stated in an article written in rationalistic *Kuḍiarasu* run by Periyār E.V. Ramaswamy. Ramalinga follows several of the Tamil *cittars* in condemning anti-sectarianism. He prescribes his new-found path of *Samarasa Śuddha Sanmārgam* laying great emphasis on *jivakāruṇyam.*

(a) *The limitations of the Scriptures and Śāstras*: It is his conviction that the Scriptures do not reveal the truth as it is but twist the same in presenting them to us. Although this tendency is typical of Tantrism, Ramalinga does not speak of the Tantric scriptures as being helpful in understanding the truth. The influence of Tamil *cittars*, including Tirumūlar and Śivavākkiyar is immense upon him although he does not acknowledge the same in his writings. His critical attitude to the scriptures can be traced back to the Tantric teachings through the Tamil *cittar* tradition which owes much to Tantrism.

Ramalinga proclaims that he was taught by the Lord the truth regarding *Vedas, Āgamas, Itihāsas* and *Purāṇas* and their cunning teachings.

> You have shown me
> the path of *Vedas* and *Āgamas*;
> the paths prescribed
> by the *Purāṇas* and *Itihāsas*;
> and thereby the cunningness implicit in them,
> You have made me understand the truth
> by your direct instruction.   (3767)

While speaking about the *Śāstras*, he comes out with the same criticism. He adds that the *Śāstras* only cause confusion. He contends that they are in no way comparable with the supreme vision of the Lord.

He proclaims that the Lord had finally taught him that all scriptures are false and futile. The Lord told him:

"My son, know the truth that all scriptures are deceptive.
See the deeds by the light of grace..."

The Lord tells him again:

"We have told you that the *Vedas* and *Āgamas* are deceptive;
the meanings of words and commentaries are lies...
Learn the truth that the *Vedas* and *Āgamas* known to the world
are sheer lies..."

However, Ramalinga pleads in one of his discourses that only in Hindu Vedas and Āgamas are taught *jñāna siddhi*. He argues that no other religion teaches these *siddhis* and deathlessness. If such teachings are to be found in them they owe their origin to Hinduism.

While making his comment on these attitudes of Ramalinga, Ooranaḍigaḷ says that Ramalinga did not completely accept the teachings of the *Vedas* and *Āgamas*; nor did he reject them in full. He adds that this attitude of Ramalinga represents the clarity of mind of a matured Śaiva Siddhānta *Sanmārgī* and *jñānī*.

(b) *Caste, Creed and Sectarianism:* Ramalinga speaks from his personal experience when he says that he was taught by the Lord that sectarian groups and their activities are childish affairs. In his earlier years he was brought up as a staunch Śaivite and he had become a radical Śaivite particularly during the last seven years of his life when he was branded as a heretic by the orthodox Śaivites. He sings boldly:

My Lord,
You instructed and told me
that many a sectarian group
founded for personal interests
and the stories told in such groups,

the way of salvation shown in them,
the visions and the deities upheld in them
are all nothing but childish affairs!   (4173)

He further adds in another verse that he was instructed by the
Lord to understand the truth that caste and colour distinctions
are sheer myth.

The four *varṇas, āśramas*
the *Purāṇas* and the rest of them
are all childish affairs indeed.
None understands well
the myth of caste and colour distinction.
Arise and see this for yourself!
        Thus you instructed me!   (4174)

Speaking about the distinctions made between the various
castes as low and high, Ramalinga comes out with his new teaching related to the coming of the Lord:

You fail to see the fact
that only those who are free
from old age and death
belong to the good caste.
You people of the world
speak of high caste and low caste.
You do see people belonging to both castes die.
Know for certain that all these polluted castes
are nothing but filthy worms.

The time has now arrived
for the advent of my father.
Come, therefore, to drink the fresh nectar
and become people of purified caste.   (5572)

Ramalinga denounces extensively in numerous verses the religious life based on caste and creed. In his recorded teachings he
stresses that caste and creed distinctions are great impediments
to improve compassion. In the small prayer which he wrote for
the use of his followers he brings in a clause of petition in which

grace is asked for to be freed from the "clutches of sects, religions and *mārgas*".

He praises the Lord who is Gracious Light and Unique Compassion as the one who is not understood by castes, religions and sects (*akaval* 115-116). He states that he was made to ascend to the highest in his spiritual form when he was freed from caste, subcaste and religion.

He calls the Lord 'the close relative' of those who have given up caste and creed.

He rebukes those who would engage themselves in vain disputes and controversies relating to the superiority of their sects over the others.

> Professing various faiths
> you expound the false Śāstras
> and shout saying:
> 'He is our God' 'He is our God'.
> But you fail to see that God is one.
> You are wiser indeed than those blind men
> who touched the elephant and disputed!
> When this body composed of five elements perishes
> what will you do?
> You do not know the means
> to make the perishable body imperishable.
> This is the time for the coming of my beloved father.
> Salvation for you has come now.
> Receive the same and rejoice. (5570)

Ramalinga condemns superstitious beliefs entertained in the established religion. In one of his verses he says that his divine mission includes destroying of such beliefs while establishing *sanmārgam* on earth:

> My Lord,
> You desired indeed
> to bury under earth
> the foolish superstitions
> which take the fictitious elements
> in the *Purānas* to be true

and establish *Sanmārgam*
at the same time.
Lord,
You endowed me with the gift of your grace
to accomplish this your purpose.   (3768)

Ramalinga's attack on cultic practices is also seen in the verses in which he condemns worship of petty deities and the practice of offering sacrifices to them. He declares that he was taught by the Lord that all the gods of the Hindu pantheon and the founders of religion have their own limitations and they are mere children compared to the One Lord who is gracious light:

"Brahmās, Rudras, Nārāyaṇas and Indras
together with the founders of faiths
like Arhat and Buddha
form only a small group of children,
who have emerged from celestial spheres
and obtained only a little light of grace
and moved about here and there
on heaven and earth
tasting the honey that was available.
Know this through the gracious Light!"
        Thus you taught me, my guru,
        the dancer king!   (4178)

In his view the band of petty gods does not merely include the local deities of popular Hinduism but also the whole of the so-called higher gods of Hinduism.

Ramalinga like Śivavākkiar condemns the practice of offering sacrifices to the local deities. During his days he encountered this practice almost at every village temple. He calls such temples the noble temples of the evil-natured petty gods. He says that he was terrified at the sight of such temples.

Like Tirumūlar and some other Tamil *cittars*, Ramalinga stresses the importance of non-killing as an essential aspect of the religious life he recommends in the name of *śuddha sanmārgam*. He would not accept meat-eaters and those who kill living beings for the purpose of eating, as members of his inner circle. He would broadly classify human beings as meat-eaters and non-meat-

eaters. The former are from the inner circle and the latter the outer
circle.

Like Paṭṭinattār and other *cittars,* Ramalinga sets the religious
life as opposed to the worldly life. But he does not attempt to
speak extensively about the physical and deplorable condition
of the body and the sex life. He speaks of the temporal and impermanent nature of human life in contrast to the glorious life without death. Stating the impermanence of life as a life in which the
relatives, parents and others, wealth and worldly affairs, are not
any real help, he persuades people to take to the *bhakti* way of
life. He denounces, in strong words, the sophisticated and cruel
life lived by the elites in society. He makes prophetic rebukes at
them and pleads with them to change their way of life. The
following verses are typical of such rebukings. Ramalinga adopts
the tone of Śivavākkiyar and Paṭṭinattār in these verses.

> You are mad people!
> You say that you live in abundance
> but would not care to think of the Lord
> with eagerness of mind and eye.
> You move about wearing fine garments
> with attendants at your service;
> but would not even look at
> the poor and hungry who come to you...   (5556)

> Your life is made up with utter lies.
> You do not realize
> that when your bodies foul and unreal
> are knocked by death
> you will go to hell as worthless worms.
> You make fun of those
> who stand before you in humility
> with mouth closed
> and hands folded in respect.
> You do not have compassion at all!
> You are meaner than the flies
> that sit on eatables dropped down.
> Do you profit anything?
> You mad people of the world!   (5564)

You commit evils unimaginable
Speak evil words hitherto not known
seek the company of undesirable people
and love to lead the most vicious kind of lives.
You would not think of the Lord
who protects you as the apple of his eye.
You would not seek him with tears!
A time will come when for the first time
you will think of those things
which you avoided all through.
And now,
do you profit anything?
You mad people of the world!   (5565)

(c) *Sanmārgam:* According to Ramalinga, religious life par excellence is *Śuddha Sanmārga.* Taking the concept of *Sanmārga* from Śaivism he modifies the same and prescribes a way of life which transcends the nature of *Sanmārgam* in Śaivism. His whole message is summarised in *Śuddha Sanmārgam* which is claimed to be the path that destroys death. Ramalinga might be called the *Siddha of Sanmārgam.* He contends that reality is known only through *Sanmārga.* Speaking to his Lord he says:

You told me my Lord
that the reality explained by
Vedānta, Siddhānta and other *antas*
could be known only in the state of
Śuddha Śhiva Śanmārga,
through great light of grace
and not by any other means.   (4179)

On the basis of this conviction he makes his appeal to the people of the world in numerous verses to follow the path of *Sanmārga.*

Impermanent indeed is everything you saw.
Defective of course, are all that you heard.
Unreal after all, is everything you learnt.
Vain indeed, are all your happiness.
You ate nothing but filth

and devoured foul food!
You worldly people
You have failed miserably
to see the truth.
No matter what you have done in the past,
obtain my father's grace
at the great dancing Hall of Wisdom
following the true path
which is *Samarasa Sanmārga*
and thus grasp clearly,
the nature of reality.
You will be rewarded indeed
with the gift of deathlessness
and you will attain joy divine.   (5579)

It is in the context of *Śuddha Sanmārga* life Ramalinga speaks
of worshipping the Lord in the form of gracious light and love.
This kind of worship is prescribed as worshipping the Lord in the
jñāna Sabai which is set in Vadalur. Also it is for the purpose of
propagating the path of *sanmārga* that he organized in 1865 the
Samarasa Veda Sanmārga Sangam. In the tradition of the Tamil
Śaiva saints and Siddhas, Ramalinga is the first one to organize
a *Sangam* over against the traditional *maḍam* where membership
is confined to a few privileged people. Ramalinga's *Sangam* is
wider in scope and offers membership to all who accept to follow
Sanmārga. While explaining the meaning of the nature of the
Sangam, Ramalinga says that *Samarasa Veda Sanmārga Sangam*
means 'the assembly of those who followed the fourth path which
is the conclusion of the book of wisdom, which is common to all
religions'. He planned to write a book with the title *Samarasa
Vēdam*. Unfortunately it was not written. If he had written the
same it would have revealed his mind. He states that all *mārgas*
are the same and makes an appeal to people to join his *Sanmārga
Sangam*. He was absolutely certain about his path soon becoming
an accepted *mārga*. The members of *Sangam* are called *Sādhus*,
meaning *Sādhakas*, "those who practice sādhana". As observed
earlier, the main objectives of the *Sangam* are teaching and prac-

tice of *Jīvakāruṇyam* and abolition of the following: meat-eating, temple sacrifices, superstitious beliefs, *jāti* and *varṇa* differences and realising the oneness of all souls in love (*Ānmaneya Orumaippāḍu*) together with the inculcation of the glorious life without death.

Ramalinga made it plain to the masses that the President of the *Sangam* was the Lord himself and those who have *Aruḷ* or compassion were its members.

Ramalinga may be called the *Sanga Siddha* among the Tamil Siddhas. He made efforts to impart his Siddhic teachings through the organisational set up of the *Sangam,* whose main task was to take the message of *Sanmārga* to the common people.

Ramalinga gives a prominent place to compassion and treating of all lives as one's own in his *Sanmārgam*. This concept is further expounded in his treatise *Jīvakāruṇya Oḻukkam,* i.e. love and goodwill towards all creatures.

— (d) *Jīvakāruṇyam:* It is an important concept in Śaivism. Tiruvalluvar who is claimed to be a Śaivite[1] has emphasized abstinence from killing and meat-eating. Tirumular also has given much importance to these in Śaiva ethics. This aspect of Śaiva ethics is so well known to the people of Tamil Nadu that they use the term *Śaivam* in ordinary speech to refer to vegetarianism. Professor P. Mutharasu[2] points out that *Jīvakāruṇyam* can otherwise be called *Ahiṃsā Dharma*. Dr. B. Natarajan[3] observes that it is what Buddha called compassion and Christ described as love. Professor V.A. Devasenapati[4] equates it with the concept of love in the writings of Albert Schweitzer. In several respects the concept is similar to *agape* (the self-giving love) spoken of in the New Testament. St. Paul's exposition of Love and the thought-provoking statements of St. John in his first epistle are worth comparing with *Jīvakāruṇyam*.[5]

---

1 Tiruvalluvar does not reveal his religious affinities in his work *Tirukkural*. The date assigned to him is first century A.D.

2 *The Life of St. Ramalinga*, Samarasa Sanmārga Sangam, Tirunelveli-6, p. 82.

3 "Economic Vision of Ramalinga", in the *Centenary Souvenir of the Sangam*, 1965, p. 89.

4 In the Foreword to Mutharasu's book, referred to above.

5 *I Corinthians*, 13; *I John* 3: 11-18; 4:20, 21.

Ramalinga explains the necessity and purpose of *Jīvakāruṇyam* in his treatise on the subject with the following words:

> The purpose of *Jīvakāruṇya Olukkam* ('observance of love towards all beings') is to remove suffering that results from hunger and killing of living beings. It should be realized that God has manifested himself in nature, in the very bodies of the living beings. When they are found to be destroyed, we should, out of *Jīvakāruṇyam* give them food and thus make those temples of the Lord shine forth in splendour.

While maintaining that one enters *Śuddha Sanmārga* by the mere practice of *Jīvakāruṇyam*, Ramalinga also describes how the *Sanmārgī* reaches the highest state of *Śuddha Sanmārga* by passing beyond several steps of spiritual experience.

Ramalinga teaches that the *Sanmārgī* has to go beyond six *antas* or ends, and so he further defines *Śuddha Sanmārga* as *Ṣaḍanta Śuddha Sanmārga*. The six *antas* mentioned by him are *yogānta, kalānta, nādānta, bodhānta, vedānta* and *siddhānta*. Some of these are classified in Śaiva Siddhānta as *Śiva tattvas*.

The *sādhaka* reaches *yogānta* by entering into *dhyāna yoga*. From there he proceeds to *kalānta*. At this state he is enabled to distinguish true wisdom from false and deceptive knowledge. He realises the worthlessness and illusory character of various religions and rituals. He also gets the knowledge of *Sanmārga*. He proceeds to the attainment of *nādānta* and realises the state of Śiva as Om.

The *sādhaka* then attains *bodhānta* where Śiva appears to him in the form of light. The *jyoti darśana* gives bliss to the soul. Ramalinga has written a number of verses on the *bodhānta* state where God is seen in the form of light. He describes this state as being within the reach of all. He formulated the watchwords *Aruṭperum Jōti; Tanipperum karuṇai* (Hail supreme Grace Light; Hail unique Compassion) as an aid for the common man to contemplate on this state. The *jyoti darśana* arranged at the *Jñāna Sabai* is also indicative of this.

The *Sādhaka* has to go beyond in his spiritual pilgrimage from *bodhānta* to *vedānta*. At this state he will find Śiva to be pure wisdom. When he passes beyond *Vedānta* to *Siddhānta*, he will come to realize his oneness of *Śuddhādvaita* state with God. The *sādhaka* then becomes *Sādhya.*

Ramalinga prays to the Lord to grant him and to all others this experience. He sings:

> Those who practise *yoga, tapas, vrata, japa* and *dhyāna* without *Jīvakāruṇyam* are not enlightened beings in the real sense of the term. They are hypocrites.

Since hunger is basic to all human suffering, those who hasten to remove it are indeed blessed persons. Ramalinga appeals to the rich to minimise expenditure on luxurious celebrations and contribute liberally for the cause of feeding the poor.

The importance of non-killing is also emphasized by Ramalinga. He vehemently condemns animal sacrifices. On the basis of non-killing Ramalinga advocates the observance of vegetarianism. He considers those who indulge in killing and meat-eating as immature beings as far the spiritual life is concerned. He sings:

> Those who kill and those who consume flesh do not belong to us. They are aliens…

Jīvakāruṇyam is affirmed by Ramalinga as a universal principle. He seeks to build upon it the brotherhood of all men which he calls *Ānmaneya Oorumaippāḍu* ('Oneness of Soul in Love'). The various *āśramas, ācāras* and controversies in matters concerning caste and sect are found to be stumbling blocks for the free exercise of *Jīvakāruṇyam* in this world. Ramalinga makes a universal appeal to all people to free themselves from these evils and practise *Jīvakāruṇyam* which is the only prerequisite for entering into *Śuddha Sanmārga* or the True Path for attaining grace.

The way of life governed and motivated by *Jīvakāruṇyam* is described by Ramalinga as *Śuddha Sanmārga.* He commends this path for all, although it is prescribed in Śaiva Siddhānta for the spiritually matured. Ramalinga is keen that *Śuddha Sanmārga* should not be confused with any secret creed. He sings:

> Many a kind of religion and many a creed has thus far spread

as sinful tenets. They have been hindrances for attaining true knowledge. Therefore, discard hereafter the evil path and embrace the new nectar, flowing from the common religion. O father, thou shouldst grant these my requests. I should know all the six *antas* and do good to all living beings. I should impart joy to all who come to me. All the worlds should turn to *Sanmārga* leaving behind vain discussions. I should, in the end, obtain thy sacred feet and be merged into it.   (4086)

In another verse he says that his request was granted and he was truly and completely changed into the very substance of the Almighty who pervaded every atom of his body.

The teachings of Ramalinga and his practical philosophy of *Śuddha Sanmārga* stand unique among the contributions to Tamil saints and sages. Coming, as he did, in the tradition of the great Siddhas who had dedicated their lives for the service of mankind, Ramalinga made social service and reform part and parcel of his religion.

His zeal in seeking the higher than the highest in religion and his message of love which gives hope to the common man to rise to the level of the so-called enlightened beings, together with the universal outlook that pervades his teachings, are challenges to orthodox Śaivism in Tamil Nadu. He has paved the way for further reform and rethinking in Śaivism.

Ramalinga certainly prepared the way for the Theosophical movement in India. Yogī Śuddhānanda Bhārati, a great scholar who had spent a number of years in the Aurobindo Ashram writes:

The Theosophical Society is an offshoot of Ramalinga's ideal of one humanity. Sri Aurobindo's *Life Divine* and *Synthesis of Yoga* breathe with the important truths discovered by Ramalinga. The descent of the Supernatural Force and the transformation of the human substance into the Divine was really an idea of Ramalinga...Mahatma Gandhi fulfilled Ramalinga's great passion for Ahimsā.[1]

---

1 Yogī Śuddhānanda Bhāratī, "The Clarion Call of Ramalingam", in the *Centenary Souvenir of the Sangam*, Madras: 1965, pp. 129-130.

Ooran Aḍigaḷ has rightly pointed out that the first one to establish a spiritual *Sangam* in Tamil Nadu was Ramalinga.

It must be stated here that Ramalinga has distinguished himself as a saintly poet of the masses. His simple, chaste and crisp style of Tamil poetry has given inspiration to the national poet Subramanya Bharati (1882-1921), who has called himself a Siddha, and a host of poets who came after him including Paṭṭukoṭṭai Kalyāṇasundaram and Kaṇṇadāsan, who have become popular through their cine songs.

IV

THE SAMARASA ŚUDDHA SANMĀRGA SANGAM

More than a hundred years have passed now since the inception of the Sangam. The centenary celebration took place in Madras on a grand scale from 11th to 13th June 1965. There is nothing remarkable in the early years of its history except the fact that meetings and conferences were conducted and the poor were fed. The then leaders of the Sangam were chiefly concerned with the reopening of the Sabai which was closed by the orders of Ramalinga in 1873. It was reopened two years after the earthly life of Ramalinga on the initiative of a Brahmin priest. He claimed that Ramalinga had appeared to him in a dream and had asked him to take action for the reopening of the Sabai. Daily and monthly *pujās* at the Sabai were introduced. The Sangam at this stage was satisfied with the regular worship at the Sabai and the feeding of the poor at the Dharmaśālai. No systematic attempt was made to spread the message of Ramalinga and thus to strengthen the organizational set-up of the Sangam.

In the early decades of the present century the Sangam received the support and sympathy of two outstanding Śaivite Tamil scholars, namely Maraimalai Adigal (Swamy Vedachalam) and Thiru V. Kalyanasundaranar. Maraimalai Adigal fought against the orthodox Śaivites who for the second time publicly denounced the writings of Ramalinga. Thiru V. Kalyanasundaranar was much influenced by Ramalinga and strove during his life-time to give popularity to the teachings of Ramalinga. He presided over the annual conference of the Sangam in 1929 at Vadalur. His presidential address which was later published is full of deep insights into the teachings of Ramalinga.[1]

---

1   *Ramalinga Swamigal Tiruvullam*, Madras: Sadhu Press, 1962 (Fourth Edition).

The Saṅgam was officially registered in the name of *Samarasa Śuddha Sanmārga Sathia Saṅgam* in 1946 with its headquarters at Vadalur. During the past twenty years the Saṅgam has had steady growth. It is estimated that there are about 138 branches of the Saṅgam in Tamil Nadu. Apart from the regular members, there are a number of sympathisers and supporters of the Saṅgam.

The main activities of the Saṅgam include organizing of conferences at state and district levels and feeding the poor at the Dharamaśālai every day and in the branches on important occasions.

The Saṅgam has taken interest in running schools and boarding homes in the Sabai campus at Vadalur. By the efforts of two leading members, O.P. Ramaswamy Reddiar (a former chief minister of Tamilnadu) and D. Perumal Chettiar, this was made possible. The latter started running five hostels, free of charge, for about two hundred boys studying in various schools. The Saṅgam published for some time the monthly *Arutcudar* edited by Turavi Kandasamy, an ascetic follower of Ramalinga. Some other journals were published from time to time from Madras, Tirunelveli and Coimbatore.

Several missionary bodies have started functioning. Two of these, Kanchi Ramalinga Mission and Siruvachiyur Ramalinga Mission, are affiliated to the Saṅgam. The Tamil Nadu Ramalinga Mission and Arutjoti Ramalinga Mission are functioning as independent bodies. The former was founded in 1950 and it runs a primary school in Vadapalani, Madras. Arutjoti Ramalinga Mission was organized at the initiative of Sri V.M. Gadigachalam, a leading lawyer and honorary magistrate.

These missionary bodies are chiefly concerned with the propagation of the teachings of Ramalinga. Arutjoti Ramalinga Mission members have several times undertaken *padayātrās,* taking the message of Ramalinga to the villagers with the purpose of organizing auxiliary Saṅgams.

Mention must be made of Sri Giridhari Prasad. He is a Gujarati by birth and has settled in Coimbatore. He is a lawyer. He is considered to be one of the able exponents of the teachings of Ramalinga. He knows about ten Indian languages and is familiar with the teachings of the saints and reformers of the north; he gives scholarly discourses, putting before the people the message of Ramalinga alongside the teachings of Kabīr, Meerā, Rāmakrishna and Vivekānanda. He has achieved remarkable fluency in expressing himself in Tamil. He is well-versed in *Tiruvaruṭpā* and several other works of devotional poetry in Tamil. He has travelled all over Tamil Nadu propagating the teachings of Ramalinga, often under the auspices of the Arutjoti Ramalinga Mission. He has also taken the message of Ramalinga to Malaysia, Burma, Ceylon and Japan. He is described by Tamilvanam, an ardent follower of Ramalinga and an accepted writer in Tamil, as the 'Vivekānanda of Ramalinga'. Tamilvanam has written a short biography of Giridhari Prasad,[1] apart from interesting articles about him[2] and the activities of Arutjoti Ramalinga Mission in his magazine *Kalkandu,* widely read in Tamil Nadu by the youth.

Some prominent politicians in Tamil Nadu are also showing interest in the propagation of the message of Ramalinga, and they actively participate in the affairs of the Sangam. Sri N. Mahalingam, an ex-Congress M.L.A., served the Sangam as one of its Vice-Presidents. Sri M.P. Sivagnanam, the founder of the Tamilarasu Kazhagam, though not a formal member of the Sangam, has participated in several of the conferences and meetings of the Sangam. He has written an excellent book on Ramalinga under the title *Vallalar Kanda Orumaippadu* ('The integration visualized by Vallalar') in which he points out the relevance of Ramalinga's teachings for the affairs of the country at the present time. He contends that Ramalinga is the greatest reformer of our times and that he was the first to speak of national integration, on the basis of which ideology universal brotherhood has to be built up. He also maintains that Ramalinga had a clear vision of a socialistic pattern of society towards which the country is moving today. This book won the President's Award. The name of Ooran Aḍigaḷ, a recent biographer of

---

1 *Giridhari Prasad,* (Madras: Manimegalai Prasuram).

2 E.g. *Kalkandu,* Ed. by Tamilvanam (16-9-1965 and 16-12-1965) 83, Purasawalkam High Road, Madras.

Ramalinga, should also be mentioned here. He had served as Town Planning Inspector for twelve years in the municipalities of Srirangam, Trichinopoly and Vellore. In 1967, on his thirtyfifth birthday, he became an ascetic. He lives in Vadalur and serves as the secretary of the Śuddha Sanmārga Nilayam in Vadalur and as a trustee of the Sabai. He has written a book on the history of Vadalur and another one about Ramalinga in Tamil. His biography of Ramalinga is considered to be the most informative among the numerous books written about him. It contains about six hundred pages.

The Samarasa Śuddha Sanmārga Sathia Sangam of the North Arcot District organized weekly lectures on the works of Ramalinga in 1966. Rasapati Adigal was expounding the cantos of *Tiruvarutpā* for two years. His lectures were printed in eight volumes. After his sudden death in January 1968, Palur Kannappa Mudaliar has continued writing commentaries for the series. Four more volumes were printed in the following year. Sri A. Balakrishnan, a lawyer and a follower of Ramalinga, took up the work of re-editing *Tiruvarutpā* after his retirement and completed it in twelve volumes. He has translated a number of poems of Ramalinga into English. These are published in the form of a book, sponsored by Arutjoti Ramalinga Mission in 1966, six years after his death.

Sri P. Mutharasu, a Śaivite Tamil scholar, has written a biography of Ramalinga in English and has translated fifty selected poems from *Tiruvarutpā*.

It is noteworthy that Christians and Muslims have also spoken from the Sangam platform paying their tributes to Ramalinga. The list of the speakers for the South Arcot District conference of the Sangam held at Vadalur from 17th to 19th January 1965 included the names of the Rev. S.W. Savarimuthu and Sri N.A. Rasheed.

It must however be stated here that there is a growing dissatisfaction among some members of the Sangam regarding its affairs. Those members of the Sangam who have a deep concern for its growth constantly point out the divisions and disunity that exist in the organization, chiefly due to difference of opinion among the leaders. Another criticism coming from within the Sangam is that it is gradually deviating from the main teachings of Ramalinga by entertaining communalism and encouraging idol worship, particularly of the image of Ramalinga. The attempts to bring together the leaders of the Saṅgam and the Missions to work out a constructive programme of activities have not yet been fruitful.

According to the information available through Sri Baghiradhan, Secretary, Ramalingar Paṇi Manram, Madras, the Manram is renewing its activities in various parts of Tamil Nadu. Although there are hundred and thirty-eight branches of the mission, only a few of them are active with any definite socio-religious programme. At a place called Chinnalapatti in Madurai District Sri Ramalinga Sanmārga Saṅgam is operating a free medical dispensary. Siddha and Ayurvedic treatment is offered free to the rural poor. At Coimbatore the Saṅgam has made an impact on the citizens by administering a daily feeding of not less than hundred poor persons. Meetings to propagate the teachings of Ramalinga and street preachings are also organised occasionally under the patronage of Sri N. Mahalingam, Chairman, Ramaligar Paṇi Manram. The other activities include free treatment to the poor at H.J. Hospital and work among drug addicts. An annual *Pādayātrā* from Madras to Vadalur is organised every year in which about hundred people participate. They march their way to Vadalur halting at a number of places to preach the message of Ramalinga to the rural folk.

The Ramalingar Paṇi Manram at Madras organises the birthday celebration of Ramalinga Swamy on 5th October every year. The celebration which continues for a week includes discourses on *Tiruvaruṭpā* and special lectures by eminent scholars.

A serious handicap for the Saṅgam is the lack of structural and organizational set-up. A few magazines and newsletters published in the past are not in circulation now and the authentic Saṅgam publications are only a few in number. The Samarasa Sanmārga Araichi Nilayam at Vadalur continues to be the only official publishing house which sends out reprints of Ramalinga's life history and *Tiruvaruṭpā*. The services of Ooran Aḍigaḷ, an ardent follower and apostle of Ramalinga, are to be highly commended. The Saṅgam has not given serious thought to engage itself in nation building activities. The pietistic tendencies are more dominant than the spirit of service. There is hope for the Saṅgam and the mission agencies to make their own contributions to the religious and social lives of the Tamils, if, like the Quakers they take to the spirit of service. By joining hands with religious movements which have similar objectives, the Saṅgam can strive to build up friendy inter-faith dialogue between them and work for maintaining communal harmony in the present day pluralistic set-up of the Indian society.

APPENDIX

(The following is a prayer written by Ramalinga Swamy for the use of the members of the Saṅgam. The Saṅgamites recite the prayer together with a few selected verses from *Tiruvaruṭpā*.)

O God who art mysterious, all-possessing and glorious Light of Grace, we beseech thee to grant unto us, that from now on our minds be kept untainted by the varying observances of religions, sects, *mārgas* and *varṇa-āśrama*. We pray thee to make the truth of Oneness of all souls in love; the chief ideal of Śuddha Sanmārga abound in us at all times and at all places. O Lord of Gracious Light, we hail thee for thy unique and gracious compassion.

SELECT BIBLIOGRAPHY

A. The Life of Ramalinga Swamy

Francis, T. Dayanandan, *Ramalinga Swamy* (English), Madras: The Christian Literature Society, 1972.

Kalyanasundaranar, Tiru V., *Ramalinga Swamigal Tiruvullam,* Madras: Sadhu Press, 1962 (Fourth Edition).

Mutharasu, P., *The Life of St. Ramalingar* (English), Tinnevely: Samarasa Sanmarga Sangam, 1961.

Ooran Adigal, *Ramalinga Adigal Varalaru,* Vadalur: Samarasa Sanmarga Aaraicci Nilayam, 1971.

Sivagnanam, M.P., *Vallalar Kanda Orumaippadu,* Madras: Inba Nilayam, 1963.

Sriraman, K., *Adigalar Arul Vazhkkai,* Mettukkuppam: Vallalar Daya Nilayam, 1964.

Suddhananda Bharathi, *Arutjodhi Vallalar,* Madras: 1940.

Vallalar Padhippagam, *Tiruvarutpragasa Vallalar,* Madras: 1963.

Vanmikanathan, G., *Saint Ramalingar,* Bombay: Bharatiya Vidya Bhawan, 1976.

Vellaivaranav, K., *Tiruvarutpa Cintanai,* Chidambaram: Manivasagar Padhippagam, 1986.

B. The Works of Ramalinga Swamy

Balakrishnan, A., *Thiru Arutpa* (English Renderings), Pollachi: Nachimuthu Industrial Association, 1966.

Chidambaram Ramalinga Swamy, *Tiruvarutpa* (Tamil) (ed.), A. Balakrishnan, Madras: Samarasa Sanmarga Sangam, 12 Volumes.

Mutharasu, P., *Hymns of Thiruvarutpa* (English), Tirunelveli: Samarasa Sanmarga Sangam, 1964.

Ramalinga Adigal, *Tiruvarutpa*, (ed.), Ooran Adigal, Vadalur: Samarasa Sanmarga Aaraicci Nilayam, 1972.

Ramalinga Adigal, *Arutperumjothi Agaval,* Vadalur: Samarasa Sanmarga Aaraicci Nilayam, 1975 (Fourth Edition).

C. Teachings of Ramalinga Swamy

Centenary Commemoration Volume, Madras: Samarasa Suddha
    Sanmarga Sangam, 1965.
Duraisamy Pillai, Avvai, *Tiruvarutpa Virivurai* (Tamil).
Palur Kannappa Mudaliar, *Tiruvarutpa Virivurai,* Vellore: North
    Arcot, Samarasa Sanmarga Sangam, 9-12 Parts, 1968-1969.
Raspati Adigal, *Tiruvarutpa Virivurai* (Tamil), Vellore: North
    Arcot, Samarasa Sanmarga Sangam, 1-8 Parts, 1966-1968.
Vazhithunai Raman, *Vallalarum Vasagarum,* Madras: Vasu
    Prasuram, 1966.
Vellaivaranar, K., *Tiruvarutpa Cintanai,* Chidambaram: Mani-
    vasagar Padhippagam, 1986.

D. The Writings of the Siddhas

Cittar Padalgal (Tamil), Chidambaram: Manaivasakhar Padhip-
    pagam, 1987.
Venugopala Pillai, M.V., (ed.), *Cittar Jñanakkovai* (Tamil),
    Madras: Premier Art Press.

E. Literature on the Siddhas

Briggs, George W., *Gorakhnath and the Kanphata Yogis,* Delhi:
    Motilal Banarsidass, 1982.
Jesudasan, G&H., *A History of Tamil Literature,* Calcutta: YMCA
    Publishing House, 1961.
Shomer, Karine & McLeod. (eds.), *The Sants,* Delhi: Motilal
    Banarsidass, 1987.
Meenakshisundaran, T.P., *A History of Tamil Literature,* Anna-
    malai Nagar: Annamalai University, 1965.
Subramania Iyer, A.V., *The Poetry and Philosophy of the Tamil
    Siddhars,* Chidambaram: Manivasakar Noolakam, 1969.
Zvelebil, Kamil V., *The Poets of the Powers,* London: Rider &
    Company, 1973.

F. General

Bhandarkar, R.G., *Vaishnavism, Śaivism & Minor Religious
    Systems,* Strassburg: Verläg Vonkarl J. Trudner, 1930.

Francis, T. Dayanandan, *Tamil Saivam* (Tamil), Madras: CLS, 1988 (Second edition).

Relevance of Hinde Ethos for Christian Presence: Madras; CLS., 1989.

Jaisingh, Herbert (ed.), *Inter-Religious Dialogue*, Bangalore: CISRS, 1967.

Kalyanasundaranar, Tiru. Vi., *Paramporuḷalladu Vāḻkkai Vaḻi* (Tamil) Madras: Sadhu Press, 1959.

Paramasivanandam, A.M., *The Historical Study of The Thevaram Hymns,* Madras: Tamilkalai Publishing House, 1982.

Ryerson, Charles A., *Regionalism and Religion: The Tamil Renaissance and Popular Hinduism,* Madras: CISRS-CLS., 1988.

G. Journals

Arutcudar, edited and published by Turavi Kandaswamy, Vadalur (Vol. 3: No. 10; Vol. 4: Nos. 3, 4, 5, 6, 7).

Arul Oil, edited by S. Muthuswamy, published by Nellai Samarasa Suddha Sanmarga Sangam, Tinnevelly Vol. 13: Nos. 4, 5.

Kalkandu edited by Tamilvanan, Kumudam Printers, Madras: 16-9-1965 and 16-12-1965.

Vallalar, edited and published by K. Nagarathnam, Madras-7. (Vol. 2: 2-12; Vol. 3: Nos. 1, 2, 3, 6, 7).

SUBJECT INDEX

INDEX OF PROPER NAMES